Constructive News

Ulrik Haagerup

CONSTRUCTIVE NEWS

AARHUS UNIVERSITY PRESS

Constructive News
© 2017 Ulrik Haagerup and Aarhus University Press

Cover by Trefold
Set and printed by Narayana Press, Denmark
Printed in Denmark 2017
Second edition, first impression

ISBN 978 87 7184 450 4

Aarhus University Press
Finlandsgade 29,
8200 Aarhus N
Denmark
www.unipress.dk

International distributors:

Gazelle Book Services Ltd.
White Cross Mills
Hightown, Lancaster, LA1 4XS
United Kingdom
www.gazellebookservices.co.uk

ISD
70 Enterprise Drive, Suite 2
Bristol, CT 06010
USA
www.isdistribution.com

For the future generations of journalists

CONTENTS

PREFACE

By Helmut Schmidt (1918-2015)

Former publisher of Die Zeit and Chancellor of the Federal Republic of Germany

Democracy is a European invention. So is the newspaper, the radio and the television. The Western world also invented the computer and the network of computers – the Internet. And globalisation has exported it all to the rest of planet Earth. It ought to be good, but it is not. This is because Western civilisation has developed into media-democracies, where often the media is more influential than the politicians. The influence of the news media is now stronger than it has ever been in the history of mankind, and as it has seemingly taken over, it can set the agenda and influence how the population sees itself and the world. Often, the media will focus mostly on the negative and superficial; perhaps this is because media people believe that is what people want and where the money is.

The consequences are many and severe. Firstly, people get a false picture of reality, and secondly, the West now suffers from a lack of leadership. Media-democracies do not produce leaders, but populists. Silvio Berlusconi comes to mind when one thinks of the kind of populists produced by media-democracy.

2,500 years ago, the ancient Greeks did not have media, nor did the ancient Romans 2,000 years ago. However, they had leaders. Arguably, the best political leaders in Europe in the last 100 years were Winston Churchill and Charles de Gaulle. They both came to power before democracy turned into media-democracy, where the constant media focus of exposure is on any politician who wants to attract votes and the attention of the masses to earn their seats.

We now see newsrooms and politicians tweeting – any story and any policy in less than 140 characters. It produces superficiality, not only in the minds of the receivers, but also in the minds of those who want to talk and impress.

This superficiality and negativity in the media has influenced politics. The lack of political leadership in the West will diminish its global influence. A change in the way in which the press operates, and a stronger focus of playing a more constructive role in our societies, is welcome.

I will soon be 95 and I am a has-been in all aspects of life, but my age makes me a realist. Ulrik Haagerup is half my age. He has the right to be an optimist, believing that it is possible to change journalism to be more inspirational and to benefit global society. I wish him the best of luck with this book. There is certainly a need for more constructive news.

Oktober 2014

INTRODUCTION

Why This Book?

*"When you change the way, you look at things ...
the things you look at change."*

Max Planck, Scientist

I am a journalist. I went into the profession of news with a very young and blurry idea of wanting to do good for society: Something like telling important stories to people to help them make up their own mind.

Slowly I became part of the news culture. On my first day at journalism school our teacher said with that voice you only get from a life of bad whisky, cigarettes and tough deadlines: "A good story is a bad story. If nobody gets mad, it's advertising." It runs in my veins.

Later I got a job as a news reporter and tried cover stories that would please my editors and colleagues, stories that could fit in a fast headline, generate quotes in other media and could win me prizes. I became part of the news culture. And I loved it.

But sometimes you happen to stand in front of the mirror, and then you must take the consequence for what you see: Either break the glass or shape up a little.

Not that I ever told lies. But at some point, I had to ask myself: Did I still work as a journalist, editor-in-chief, and news director for the biggest news organisation in my country in order to do good for society, or had my ambition in reality slowly changed into pleasing the news culture? And what good did it do?

Not that nobody before had told me and the rest of the news

business that we were on the wrong track. But we – journalists and editors – are not very good at being criticised. We are used to stone-walling anyone trying to influence our reporting. So when politicians criticise us for focusing too much on the negative sides of society and haunt their every mistake, we know that they just want to avoid our critical questions and attack our independent watchdog reporting.

When CEOs and interest groups ask us also to report on their suc-cesses and not only their failures, we say "buy an ad", which is also intended to embarrass them. What do they take us for, PR agents or advertising sales people?

When professors write reports on the negative bias of the press and warn of the consequences, we ignore them, because what do those intellectuals from the elite in their ivory towers know about real jour-nalism anyway?

And when our neighbour explains that she has now stopped buy-ing the newspaper and quit watching the late-night news, we start explaining to this stupid woman that it's an obligation of any adult and good citizen to follow the news.

People say that you hear the truth from children and drunk people: "Dad, sometimes you need to listen louder," my youngest teenage daughter told me one evening, as I spent my time as a father telling her were not to go, which drinks not to drink, when to be home and which boys not to kiss.

Listen louder? I had never heard that expression before. Fathers – just like journalists and editors – are much better at talking than at listening.

But if we had paid attention outside the newsroom, what would we have heard years ago?

When being asked about the trust in different professions, people in my country (and probably yours too) place journalists just bet-ween used-car sales people and real estate agents, which is an an-nual surprise to us, because we normally tell each other at our news conferences that we are in the "trust business". But we usually find comfort in the fact that politicians are even further down on the list. And then we talk about that instead.

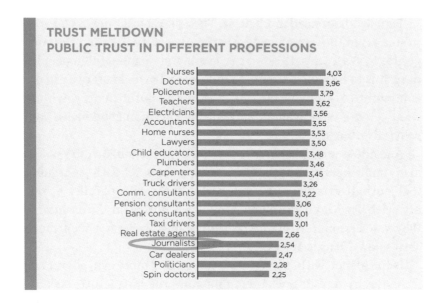

TRUST MELTDOWN
PUBLIC TRUST IN DIFFERENT PROFESSIONS

Profession	Score
Nurses	4,03
Doctors	3,96
Policemen	3,79
Teachers	3,62
Electricians	3,56
Accountants	3,55
Home nurses	3,53
Lawyers	3,50
Child educators	3,48
Plumbers	3,46
Carpenters	3,45
Truck drivers	3,26
Comm. consultants	3,22
Pension consultants	3,06
Bank consultants	3,01
Taxi drivers	3,01
Real estate agents	2,66
Journalists	2,54
Car dealers	2,47
Politicians	2,28
Spin doctors	2,25

If you do what you have always done, you'll probably end up with the same result you have always gotten. And by now most news people must have found out that our results are not good. As my group of news people, who were gathered in Dubai at World Economic Forum Global Council on the Future of Journalism, concluded back in 2008:

"The revolution in information and communication technology has probably hit no other sector harder than the news media itself. Hardly any other industry is finding its role challenged so fundamentally, its values and worth being eroded and its business model threatened to a point of extinction." To put it bluntly: Houston, we have a problem.

It is time to remember that the word "crisis" is an old Greek word for turning point. Before the discovery of antibiotics, a patient with infection would probably get well, if the fever dropped after five days. If the temperature continued to rise after day five, the patient most likely would die. That point on day five was called "crisis". So crises are good if you survive them. And we have now come to a turning point in the media world. And the cure is not new apps, faster deadlines and more of the same with less money.

People do not need more news. They need better news. Our road to success in the news business is not to beat Twitter and the competitor by 8 seconds. It is to be relevant and meaningful in people's lives. It is to become a friend, a guide and a trusted authority in our communities. And you can only become an authority if you know what you are talking about and put the common good above your own self-interest.

And no: As journalists, we really don't know enough. And yes: Too many publishers have been affected by business-school logic arguing, that journalism is just a product to be sold. So, if people click on reality celebrity Kim Kardashian, they'll get more Kim Kardashian. If they watch crime, terror, wars and hurricanes, we'll serve them more. That's news. This is our world. Or is it?

Is the planet, with its 195 countries, getting more evil, poorer and more terrifying? Or does the public miss the big picture, because we – the news media – focus only on the few important trouble spots?

Journalism is not stenography – it is the best obtainable version of the truth, as Watergate reporter Carl Bernstein once told me. Since then I have made a habit of evaluating the journalistic material in the in-flight magazines on the plane to a new country. In these magazines, the sky is always blue, the snow is new, the sun is bright, the food fantastic, the investments promising, and the girls beautiful and smiling just as much as the air hostesses and the president of the airline. It might not all be a lie, but does this kind of journalism provide a true picture of life there?

Not if I compare it with the newspapers I routinely buy at the airport, or the news I watch at the hotel on national TV. Death, murders, accidents, wars, demonstrations, political fights, accusations of corruption, wrongdoing, and all kinds of problems welcome me and normally make me regret that I came in the first place. Does this kind of traditional news journalism really provide the best obtainable version of the truth? Or is the picture we in the news media industry pass on to readers, listeners, viewers, and to our societies just as short sighted and false as the glossy magazines full of commercial journalism disguised as reporting?

Why is the news media so negative? What are the consequences? Does it do society any good? Does a good story have to be a bad story? Can we save journalism by helping it save the world? How can we improve before it is too late? These questions have fascinated me for most of my 35-year long journalism career in the news industry.

This book is the search for answers. It argues that good reporting is seeing the world with both eyes. Not missing the important stories about Ebola in West Africa, hunger, bombings in Gaza and Ukraine and millions on the run from terror and war in Syria. But also seeing stories that can inspire and engage because they show the opposite; things that work, people doing something extraordinary to solve important problems. The big picture.

Readers, listeners and viewers turn their backs on traditional media in their millions, and one of the reasons for the fundamental crisis is that people are sick and tired of the negative picture of the world presented to them by the press. Most news stories in traditional media are focused on conflict, drama, crooks and victims, and the result is neither to the benefit of the press, journalism nor the societies that we – the men and women of the press – claim to serve.

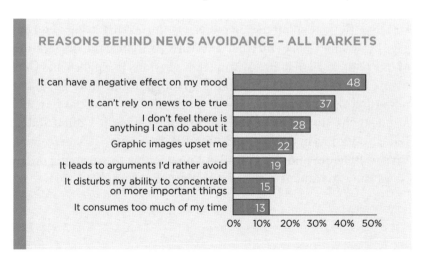

Source: Reuter's Institute for the Studies of Journalism at Oxford University: Digital News Report 2017

Reuters Institute for the Studies of Journalism at Oxford University published a new world-wide study in the summer of 2017 on the reasons why millions of people turn their backs on traditional news media.

The number one reason – 48 percent of all answers in all countries surveyed – was this: "News can have a negative effect on my mood."

Number two was that people didn't trust the news to be true, and the third reason was "I don't feel there is anything I can do about it."

So if I and my collegues in the news business think that our hard work is to the benefit of society, but in contrast we create depression, distrust and apathy, who should change?

The old newsroom saying: 'If it bleeds, it leads', is outdated. Tabloidisation of news, even in so-called serious print media, online and television news shows, has gone too far.

Thomas Patterson, Bradlee Professor of The Government & the Press at Harvard University's Kennedy School of Government, puts the problem like this: "The real bias of the press is not that it's liberal. The bias is a preferred preference for the negative."

This book is a handbook of inspiration on how we can do better in the newsrooms, in the public debate and in our democracies. Constructive News is about tomorrow: News stories that inspire and engage in a public debate for a better future. And since the first edition of this book in Danish in 2012 and new versions in English and German, Constructive News is picking up momentum. More and more newsrooms around the world – from the BBC, to The Guardian, the Minneapolis Star Tribune, the Huffington Post in the United States, Danish TV2, Swedish Radio and TV, NRK in Norway, RUV in Iceland, VRT in Belgium and Yle in Finland now follow the example of DR News and experiment with constructive news formats.

CONSTRUCTIVE JOURNALISM IN COMPARISON

	Breaking	Investigative	Constructive
Time:	Now	Yesterday	Tomorrow
Goals:	Speed	Blame	Inspiration
Questions:	What? When?	Who? Why?	What now? How?
Style:	Dramatic	Critical	Curious
Role:	Police	Judge	Facilitator
Focus:	Drama, conflict	Crooks, victims	Solutions, Best practice

Source: Constructive Institute 2017

Our democracies are now facing the largest trust meltdown on a global scale since World War II. And the public sense of failed systems is not mainly found in Russia, China or India, as most of us would like to think: Surveys on public trust in the democratic institutions by the British-based global opinion poll company Ipsos Mori found in 2017 the lowest scores in the United States, Western Europe, Brazil, South Africa and Australia.

In societies with no authorities left, the rudest, the loudest and the one with most likes will become president.

The Director General of the United Nations, Michael Moeller, who serves on the advisory board of Constructive Institute, is alarmed by the situation and calls for action:

"We live in a world where the flow of information and the possibilities for citizen participation have never been greater. Yet, many feel disempowered by the news, are disappointed in their political leadership and disengaged from decision-making. This generates a democratic deficit through apathy and indifference. It is often said that we get the media and the political leaders we deserve. It is our shared responsibility to ensure that we get the best. Because that is how we are all empowered. "Constructive News" is a welcome call for a more profound reflection about priorities and choices, not just among media professionals and political leaders, but for all of us."

Another global leader, Pope Francis, looks at the global challenge in this way:

"We have to break the vicious circle of anxiety and stem the spiral of fear resulting from a constant focus on "bad news". This has nothing to do with spreading misinformation that would ignore the tragedy of human suffering, nor is it about a naive optimism blind to the scandal of evil."

In a powerfully worded message in the beginning of 2017, the Pope said he wanted to encourage media professionals to engage in "constructive forms of communication that reject prejudice" and help create a world of "realism and trust."

Enough is Enough

Jodie Jackson would agree. She was a young woman selling perfume in her town in the Midlands, UK, when she got frustrated with the constant negative bombardment from news media surrounding her.

She wrote down her feelings in a poem, and her boyfriend helped her turn it into a video rap, which she sent to me, as she had heard that I was a media professional sharing her frustrations. I watched it at work at DR, and right after I knew what I needed to do. Jodie Jackson's poetic news consumer outcry went like this:

The purpose of the news is to engage and inform,
empower people and bring about reform,
but their words are being lost by the noise of the storm.

We hear about disaster, murder, conflict and violence,
And after a while this becomes white noise, like silence.
But when there is a bias for the negative, we lose becoming sensitive
And instead we become emotionally dead.

You see
    this negativity has been shown to be destructively informing me
Dividing me from society by creating this fear and anxiety,
For many they watch helplessly as if we are damned to be,
but that's not the only story of the fate of our humanity.

Let's hear about progress, acknowledge solutions,
This excess of negativity it's like mental pollution.
When we see good news, it's misrepresented:
We hear cats being saved from trees and the conversation is ended.
Saved instead for "and finally".

But finally, these
    stories of possibility are shown to be a vital story for society.
We need to know about how problems are being solved, issues resolved
For the sake of our souls,
Not for ignorant bliss, but because we are better than this.

We don't need sugar coating or positive spins.
Again, that's the cynical view that this conversation underpins.
And don't get it confused with entertainment, PR or fluff.
Enough is enough.

It's rigorous journalism reporting on progress.
Reporting on problems, but not ignoring success.
We publicise failure, corruption and shame,
But when it comes to human potential it's not treated the same,
And the hypocrisy is killing me.

Are you kidding me?
They point the finger at every other industry, but leave them be
As this excess of negativity
    increases velocity, atrocity, chasing more controversy.
But where is the nobility in preying on morbid curiosity?

I feel cheated,
    defeated by newspaper allegiance to profits and click baits
Regardless if it generates hate and drums up the nation
    into a fearful state.
Some people find it too much to take.
And then the stories become lost, because people switch off.

But if we want a nation that's engaged and informed
    it's time to reform.
Make a new norm, empower, inspire.
Help us achieve higher, report the good in other people.
Not just replay their evil.

If we witness the unbelievable, it makes it more achievable,
A solution seems more feasible, the only option now is to freeze or fall.
After all the truth of the world includes the good and the sad
The happy and sad.
So why would you just tell one half of the story?

It leaves us in mourning unable to see that the new day is dawning.
The power lies in us becoming aware,
To ensure they can take more care about the stories they tell
when we look at the world out there.
And why should we care?

Because the truth is that the news is an organisation
    that'sintrusive of our minds
And it's a matter of time before their words become our thoughts
Shaping our opinions more and more.

So what we are asking for, as I said before,
Is rigorous journalism reporting on progress
Reporting on problems, but not ignoring success.

It may sound idealistic. It's been labelled naïve.
But let me assure you this is not an ignorant plea.
The research says it's obvious, and to ignore it is preposterous.

So it's time for the consumers to take a stand
Because the industry will listen to us ...

Jodie Jackson, 2016

You can watch the powerful video on YouTube, if you search for Jodie Jackson and "Publish the Positive". When I had seen it, I knew I had to quit my job as news director after 10 years to try to change myself and my own profession. It was not enough to change the news culture of the Danish public broadcasting, DR, do talks and write books in my spare time.

We need a global constructive movement. We need a wakeup call to a paralysed media industry infected by cynicism. We need to understand that constructive news is neither an alternative to critical watchdog journalism nor is it an argument for harmless positive news. We need good reporting, which can inspire to possible solutions to the problems facing society, giving way to a new and more meaningful role for journalism: Not only documenting problems and finding who is to blame for them, but also facilitating dialogues in our communities on how they might be solved.

That's why we have created Constructive Institute, which opened in the summer of 2017 as an independent non-profit organisation located on the campus of the modern Aarhus University in Denmark's second biggest city. Coincidentally, in the same year, Aarhus hosted the European Capital of Culture 2017 with the theme "Rethink". And the goal of Constructive Institute is indeed to help rethink journalism.

The mission is as simple as it is naïve: We want to change the global news culture in five years. Funded by philanthropy, Constructive Institute will follow three roads to that global change:

1. New Knowledge: research in partnership with respected scientists on political science, psychology and media, educational material for future journalists, and innovation of new constructive media concepts, so that not only the entertainment industry is successful in creating global concepts for the mass audience (X-Factor, Britain's Got Talent, Dancing with the Stars), but serious issues facing society can also become engaging and solution focused.

2. New Inspiration: keynotes, conferences, seminars, masterclasses, global prizes and helping boards revise strategies and assisting editors and journalists implement a more constructive news culture.

3. New Role Models: giving the best talents in the news business a year as Constructive Fellows at Aarhus University – like the John S. Knight Fellowship at Stanford University and The Nieman Fellowship at Harvard. In Aarhus, six Danish and (from 2018) hopefully six international fellows not only have access to the newest scientific knowledge on their beat, but they can also explore possible solutions to the major challenges facing society while they get a year-long education on constructive storytelling.

You might not be successful in changing everybody else. But one thing you can do: Change your own mindset and behaviour. Be a role model for others to follow. And if you ask better questions, you might get better answers.

I'm convinced that just as journalism is partly responsible for some of the problems facing democracy, journalism must also be a major part of the solution. Who else should people turn to get the best obtainable version of the truth? But then we must dare to change.

I thank talented editors, CEOs, politicians, reporters, scholars, present and lost media users for sharing their frustrations, ideas and hopes. I'm proud to have had Jakob Vestergaard from Aarhus University Press and journalist Johanne Haagerup as editors for this revised edition with a professional eye on both structure and details. I'm grateful to my friends, family and the great people around Constructive

Institute and Aarhus University for inspiration and for believing in better media to the benefit of society.

This is Constructive News. Let's make journalism great again.

Aarhus, October 2017
Ulrik Haagerup
Journalist, founder and CEO
Constructive Institute

PART 1

IDENTIFYING THE PROBLEM

Chapter 1

WHAT'S WRONG?

You better start swimmin'
Or you'll sink like a stone.
For the times
they are a-changin'.

Bob Dylan, Singer-songwriter

Fake news is not the real problem. News is. Misinformation and false stories from state supported hackers, immoral interest groups and teenagers finding cynical ways to make a living online is indeed Roundup for public trust. The new thing is mainly the speed at which these stories can spread in the digital world. But it is not really new.

When the American president John F. Kennedy visited Dallas in Texas in 1963, he had a speech in his inner pocket. But before he had a chance to read it, he was assassinated. What did we miss? What would he have said?

The manuscript was later found in the president's blood-stained jacket. So here is the warning Kennedy never had the chance to give to the world:

"Ignorance and misinformation can handicap this country's security. In a world of complex and continuing problems, in a world full of frustrations and irritations, America's leadership must be guided by the lights of learning and reason — or else those who confuse rhetoric with reality and the plausible with the possible will gain the popular ascendancy with their seemingly swift and simple solutions to every world problem."

54 years later, the world is still trying to understand how the most powerful democracy in the world elected a politically inexperienced, boastful construction billionaire into the White House.

The three most important stories in my more than 35 years in journalism are the fall of the Berlin Wall, 9/11, and the election of Donald Trump. A lot of analysis has been made on the historic event which brought communism to a peaceful end in 1989, and on why Islamic terrorists brought down the symbol of capitalism, as they did when they flew passenger planes into the Twin Towers of the World Trade Center in 2001. But the election of Donald Trump in 2016 is still a puzzle.

What happened? Was he brighter than the other candidates? Was his policy coherent, clearly demonstrating an alternative approach? Or was this multi-billionaire simply riding on the crest of a wave because of a tremendous campaign budget?

Had German statesman and former Federal Chancellor of West Germany, Helmut Schmidt, still been with us, he would probably have emphasised an even scarier answer. To the very last, Schmidt, who died in November 2015, was the publisher at the successful German weekly, Die Zeit. This was where I met him in 2014 in connection with research for the first edition of this book on the relationship between media and politics.

Helmut Schmidt spent most of his life on the observation and description of, and participation in, democracy. And he received me in the same office, crammed with books and yellow-tinged press cuttings, as he did when I last visited him in the late 1980s, putting what became the end of the cold war into words for an article in my newspaper. 25 years later, his wrinkles deepened a little, the brushed-back hair considerably greyer, and the walls of the Hamburg office grown more tar-brown after another couple of decades of chain smoking. Thus, considering the long pause after my first question, I feared for a moment that my long drive south on the E45 from Denmark to Germany had been in vain. But then the 95-year-old sucked the life out of yet another Reyno Menthol, exhaled, and answered:

"Democracy is a European invention. So is the very idea of media. And we have exported democracy as well as media to the rest of the world. This ought to be a good thing. But it isn't," Helmut Schmidt said.

"Because today the western democracies have developed into

media democracies, and the media's influence is stronger than ever before in the history of mankind. The media are setting the agenda, deciding how populations perceive themselves and the world. Often, our main focus is on the negative and the shallow – maybe because media people believe this to be what people want, and where the money is. But the consequences are many, and they are serious. Primarily, because populations get a false picture of reality. Secondly, because the West is now suffering from lack of leadership," Schmidt continued, before playing his trump card:

"Media democracies do not create leaders, they create populists."

Schmidt mentioned another construction billionaire, the now scandalised former Italian prime minister Silvio Berlusconi, who epitomises the type of populist who will be elected in media democracies. I cannot help wondering who he would have mentioned had he lived long enough to follow the 2016 American presidential campaign.

"The media loves me"

Certainly, Schmidt's analysis was razor sharp: In our modern media democracies, we run the risk that politicians become more focused on securing their own election or re-election than on providing solutions to societal challenges 5 or 10 years ahead. And spin doctors and media consultants will advise anyone chasing election to target their speech at the media's news criteria. So, when the media angle their content towards conflicts, drama, victims and villains, the headlines will go to the candidate who is best at creating conflict and drama, and who divides the world into easily recognisable villains and victims.

Muslims are terrorists, my opponents are morons, Mexicans are rapists, you are losers, but I'll make you into winners. Vote for me.

As Trump himself declared during his campaign: "The media loves me."

According to a count performed by The Tyndall Report, the Trump campaign did indeed attract more media exposure all through the year 2015 than all the democratic candidates combined. And in 2016 Trump averaged a quarter of the overall political coverage by the major newscasts of the three television networks – ABC, CBS and NBC – combined.

According to evaluations by the independent Swiss media research institute, Media Tenor, which processes statistical data of news-media content, the marketing value of the media coverage ran into 1.9 billion USD during 2015 – an amount which by far exceeded Trump's direct campaign fund and gave him a gargantuan commercial advantage in his race against the other republican presidential candidates.

When even so-called serious media applies a tabloid journalism approach, the tendency is that the political debate will be shaped accordingly. In early 2016 the American TV network CBS was criticised for overexposing Donald Trump broadcasting live TV from almost all his campaign meetings. The answer from CEO Leslie Moonves highlights what has gone wrong with journalism:

"It may not be good for America, but it's damn good for CBS. ... The money is rolling in. Bring it on, Donald. Go ahead. Keep going."

And so he did.

The question remains as to whether journalism has been abducted by business-school logic, claiming that journalism is nothing but a product to be marketed. That the "customer" is always right. That what is measurable will be measured. The risk is that when important matters are not measurable, the measurable will then become important. Because it is much easier to measure market share, readership, page exposures and listening time than it is to determine whether the journalism we provide is to the benefit of society, makes people wiser and provides them with a better opportunity to make choices of their own.

It is not only in American newsrooms that the need for self-examination appears. As a news trade, we now need to ask ourselves whether we have created an internal culture to promote media democracy, which will again engender political populism and citizens left with a warped picture of reality.

We need to bring journalism back to its publicist roots. To a journalistic approach intent on creating understanding more than helping people to kill time. Where money is earned for providing journalism – not the other way around. Where you care about the society you serve – and not just say so. And where you remember that responsible journalism is not just about whom to blame, and looking with one eye aimed only at confirming the angle you started with in your research.

Embarrassing questions

There are some embarrassing questions to my beloved, yet distressed profession, which urgently require answers:

- Are we the ones who created Trump and others like him?
- Is this because populism speaks directly into our news criteria that love the crude and the rude, the attacking, the non-conforming, the outrageous approach? Because to a media trade under pressure, an entertaining fight is faster, cheaper and easier to cover than content which requires things as old-fashioned as documentation, the checking of facts and, not forgetting, research?
- Is serious journalism lost on an ever-increasing part of the voters who have ceased to trust traditional media and instead seek confirmation of their world view through friends and acquaintances on social media?

The secret algorithms of social media giants have proved to favour posts which talk to the heart rather than the head. A post on Facebook that generates pure joy or hate spreads much faster and wider than nuances and balanced reporting – changing news media into views media.

Global mental obesity pandemic

Why do more and more people become fat? Because the empty calories are so easy to find: There are french fries on every street corner, Coca-Cola in the vending machines in the public schools and aisles after aisles of chips, candy and chocolates in the supermarket.

Now we are also moving towards a global mental obesity pandemic because the "empty calories" of content have become so easily accessible, and because it requires true effort on the part of the individual to digest in-depth articles, watch television documentaries, let alone read a book. It is much easier to kill time on a series on Netflix, check updates on Facebook, and play violent games on the PlayStation.

Trump and others like him are the result of the credibility meltdown that strikes when large parts of the population no longer have faith in the political elite. Either because they experience that there is a difference between what politicians promise to do and what they actually do. Or because visions and political content are replaced by rhetorical dodging, tactics and positioning.

Daniel Korski was advisor to the then British Prime Minister David Cameron during the Brexit vote. Korski has explained exactly when 10 Downing Street realised that "Remain" would lose the referendum to "Leave". It was when they understood how the news media was covering the debates on for the decision that lay before Britain: to keep the status quo and stay with the EU, or to take a risk, stepping out onto the potentially thin ice on the journey towards independence.

In one corner, 90 professors and ice experts, who all said that with their expertise, science and research on the breakpoint of ice, it would not be advisable for the nation to go out there. The ice was too thin and would break. In the other corner, and with equal airtime, was a 51-year-old crystal healer from Sheffield, who knitted her own tampons, and who told the media and the voters that she could feel that it was right and safe for Britain to walk out on that ice. And she also thought that those professors and politicians were very elitist. (My interpretation and exaggeration).

"When facts and feelings are presented as equal, facts will lose," Daniel Korski said to Danish media Zetland. This comes as no surprise for the experienced Danish member of parliament, Peter Skaarup, from the successful and powerful Danish People's Party. He publicly announced in August 2017, that "in politics there is no correct answer – only feelings and attitudes."

"I think that facts are not as important as our attitudes and feelings. It can be useful to know the facts. But in a political debate, how we choose to act depends more on our feelings and our perception of the problems," Peter Skaarup, who is also the chairman of the Legal Affairs Committee, explained to the Danish daily Politiken.

At the political festival Folkemødet in the summer of 2017, Peter Skaarup participated in a debate with the CEO of a security company, and they explained how they worked to fight crime with expensive security systems for private homes and with being "tough on crime" respectively – without once mentioning the fact that the risk of being a victim of a criminal act in Denmark has rapidly declined in recent years.

Perception of reality

Journalism is the filter between reality and the perception of reality. How are we doing, then? Comprehensive surveys demonstrate a huge gap between facts and populations' perception of facts:

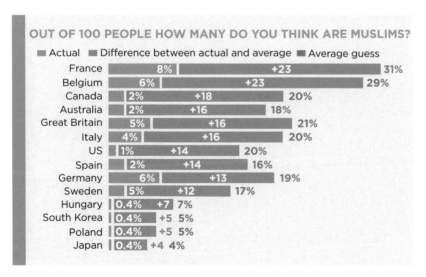

Source: Ipsos Mori and The Guardian 2015

In 2015, global analysis company Ipsos Mori found a huge gap between reality and the public perception of reality. Italians believe almost half of the Italian population to be unemployed. Unemployment rates for 2014 equalled 12 percent. Americans read and watch so many stories about teenage pregnancies that they believe every fourth woman aged between 13 and 19 become pregnant. The factual statistic is three in a hundred.

The fact is that people – and among them our leaders – make decisions based not on facts, but what they believe to be the facts. Or what they want the facts to be. Just before the United States presidential election between Trump and Clinton in November 2016, the American unemployment rate dropped to 4.9 percent, which was the lowest in 9 years and an indication of fast American economic growth. But the average American – democrat and republican – thought that the unemployment rate was 31 percent. If you think that almost one third of your countrymen are unemployed, who do you vote for? She who claims it's going better, or he promising to Make America Great Again?

In France, the average Frenchman believes that 31 percent of the French population are now Muslims. The actual figure is below 9 percent. But if you believe that one third of the people in your country are Muslims, and the only Muslims you know are those blowing themselves and others up in the news all the time, who do you vote for?

In Denmark, crime rates are falling and have been doing so for years. But people feel more and more insecure in their lives. When we ask them why, they answer:

"Because of all the murders, the terror, the home robberies, the shootings and it's getting worse and worse!"

"Do you mean in your town?"

"No," they say, "in the news. On my 24-hour news channel, on the internet, on my phone, on the front pages, the billboards, it's everywhere."

The Danish Ministry of Justice published in the late summer of 2017 a survey among 900 Danes, who were asked if they thought that recent years had shown more or fewer car thefts, burglaries, robberies and crimes by the young. 80 percent – and mainly women – gave the wrong answer, as they were sure crime was getting worse or stayed the same.

Police inspector Michael Kjelgaard from the National Investigation Center explained in the Danish newspaper Politiken:

"The stream of information is now so huge that almost every crime is being mentioned on social media or in the news media. We do try to create a balance by reporting on the facts of the drop in crime. But it just doesn't have such a big impact, as it is not being covered in the media as much as the few spectacular crime events, which take up time and space in the news. Therefore, many get the impression that things are getting worse, even though the opposite is the case."

Recently, Kristeligt Dagblad – a Danish daily – covered a national survey, demonstrating that Danes believe over a third of the world population to be without access to clean drinking water, whereas the accurate figure is 9 percent. The truth is this: Never before in human history have so few people lost their lives in warfare as is the case right now, in spite of the calamitous situation in Syria. Nonetheless, most surveys show that never before have we felt so unsettled. Could it be that the media are under the misapprehension that a good story can only be an unhappy one, forgetting the nuances and the overall picture?

As Bill Gates, former CEO of Microsoft and now a philanthropist once put it:

"The world is steadily becoming a better place to be. But this is not covered by the media, as no one will call a press conference about those children who did NOT die from malaria."

Don't Panic

Close your eyes and think for a moment of the word Africa. What do you see? People starving, children dying from diseases, mothers infected with HIV, endless wars, depression and little hope will be the answer to many. Because this is what is being reported by our news media supported by help organisations and NGO campaigns trying to get our attention, our sympathy and our money. Not that it is wrong that hunger is still a problem in areas when harvest fails. Not that it is false that malaria and AIDS still kill thousands. Not that it is wrong that civil wars in Sudan, the Democratic Republic of Congo and the Central African Republic are terrifying and seem to go on and on. But is that the full picture of a continent of one billion people?

Hans Rosling, a Swedish professor who devoted his statistical skills to get the facts of the world straight, spent his last years explaining to the world, that they have the wrong idea about Africa. Few people know that East African countries, such as Rwanda, experience a growth rate of their GNP similar to China's. That the middle class has doubled in Africa south of the Sahara. That more and more governments of African countries now change not due to revolution, but due to the results of democratic elections. And that diabetes is becoming a bigger problem than AIDS in many African countries, where obesity is more widespread than starvation.

In one of Rosling's speeches for the United Nations, titled 'Don't Panic' (also published on his independent website gapminder.org) he stated that "The differences between different areas in Africa are huge. But in general Africa is really improving. Child mortality is decreasing rapidly, life expectancy is growing rapidly and so is the number of people who can read and write."

As a professor at the Karolinska Institute in Stockholm, Rosling began to test his students and fellow professors' knowledge on the basic facts of the world. And it turned out that they performed worse than a test group of chimpanzees, which means worse than random. "Such wrong answers could not be the results of guessing. They must be due to preconceived ideas that in a systematic way create and maintain ignorance. Only preconceived ideas can make us perform worse than random," explained the professor.

His organisation, Gapminder, has tested the knowledge of the general population in Sweden, the United Kingdom, and the United States, using large opinion polls representing the total population in three countries who normally consider themselves blessed with an educated and literate public. The answers are interesting.

The population in all three countries turn out to be sure, that the average number of children per woman in the world is 4.5. The true number is 2.5. Two thirds of the population in those three countries believed that poverty in the world has doubled since the early 1990s. The fact is that according to the World Bank, the number of people living in poverty globally has been almost halved in the last 30 years – the lowest ever in the history of mankind.

People were asked how many children United Nations experts expect there to be in the world by the year 2100. They could choose between two, three or four billion children. Less than seven percent of the American population had the correct answer, that the United Nations expects no increase in the number of children in the world, which is now two billion. The reason is that birth control is widespread, wealth is growing, and that the United Nations and national programs to reduce the number of children, have had a massive effect. In 40 years, the number of children per woman in one of the most populated countries in the world, Bangladesh, has dropped from seven to two.

"Statistical facts don't come to people naturally. Quite the opposite," Rosling explained before he died in 2017. "Most people understand the world by generalising personal experiences which are very biased. In the media, the 'news-worthy' events exaggerate the unusual and put the focus on swift changes. Slow and steady changes in major trends don't get much attention. The danger is that we, and our politicians, make the wrong decisions if we base them on a false picture of the world."

In 2014, I invited Rosling to make a talk to the staff at Danish Public Broadcasting, DR. Then I had an idea: What if he was being interviewed by one of our news anchors? The result was astonishing, and the interview we put online afterwards is still DR's most watched clip ever with more than 12 million views – in a country with 6 million people.

"You say that the world is getting better. But seen from a media perspective the world is full of wars, conflicts, chaos ..."

"No, no, no! That is completely wrong," Rosling interrupted and smashed his right foot up on the white polished news desk.

"If you choose to only show my shoe, it is ugly, and it gives one picture of me. If you show all of me, you get another picture. The world is much more nuanced that you present it."

"How do you know that?" the skeptical news anchor asked.

"From the United Nations and the World Bank. There is nothing to discuss, and it is not controversial at all. I'm right. And you are wrong."

Takeaway

The Path from Traditional Journalism to Constructive News

- Not more, but better
- Not negative, but critical
- Not angry, but curious
- Not accusatory, but inspiring
- Not tabloid, but entertaining
- Not populist, but popular
- Not dull, but modern
- Not only ask the traditional "where", "who", and "when", but add the "how" and the "what now"

Chapter 2

WHY ARE YOU SO NEGATIVE?

Tell me, why is the media here so negative? Why?

A.P.J. Abdul Kalam, Indian President 2002-2007

The truth is: We know. Just about every time we – publishers, editors, reporters and other members of the press – happen to talk to people outside of our profession, we get asked: "Why are you always so negative?"

We answer instinctively: "We're not negative, we're just journalists", and then we follow up with a very long explanation with the simple point that journalism is about dealing with reality, and just imagine if we stopped covering stories like terrorists flying passenger planes into tall buildings to avoid being negative. That usually shuts people up for a while.

For years, newsroom culture has been strong and easy to follow: Critique is the preferred social interaction and a philosophy of life. The person critiquing is brighter than the rest, and as early as journalism school we learn that we are part of the ruling class who should reveal corruption, fight perpetually against the untamable greed among the elite. Uncover problems. Criticise power. The Fourth Estate. The chosen few. Here we come. This is how we were going to shake the world.

We loved to quote the greatest in the profession, like the former editor of The Sunday Times in London, Harold Evans, who said: "Before interviewing a politician always ask: Why is this bastard lying to me?"

We watched 'All the President's Men' on video, where the heroes of our new profession looked like Dustin Hoffmann and Robert Redford, and we understood what journalism could and should do: It can topple presidents, if only we were as smart, as diligent and as uncompromising as Bob Woodward and Carl Bernstein – and looked closely enough for a Deep Throat. One problem arose pretty soon: We do not have any presidents in the Kingdom of Denmark. But then we had to settle for CEOs, ministers, members of parliament, lawyers, policemen, priests and everybody else with authority and a tie.

Look at the words describing the nominees for the American Pulitzer Prize 2015 in the category news:

- "... a riveting series that probed why South Carolina is among the deadliest states in the union ..."
- "... digital account of a landslide that killed 43 people ..."
- "... the influence of lobbyists can sway congressional leaders and state attorneys general, slanting justice toward the wealthy and connected."
- "... widespread corruption ..."
- "... security lapses [in The Secret Service] ..."
- "... a painstaking, clear and entertaining explanation of how so many U.S. corporations dodge taxes ..."
- "... vivid human stories on Ebola in Africa ..."
- "... nuanced portraits of lives affected by [California's] drought ..."
- "... wrongful conviction and other egregious problems in the legal and immigration systems."
- "... savvy criticism ..."
- "... expose the ... the human costs of income inequality"
- "... the despair and anger in Ferguson, MO ..."
- "... Ebola epidemic in West Africa."

Any of these stories are great. But the point is, that covering these kinds of problems are the only way you normally win a prize for news journalism.

A real news story must, traditionally, be about a conflict, a drama, a crook or a victim. And for it not to be boring, it should be written in a short, square style and without too many shades of grey. That is the way the bloodhounds out there want it, and that is the way that they would get it. Because that's how journalism is, and this is how we have done it for as long as anyone can remember.

Take a look at the list of the winners of the Danish equivalent of the Pulitzer Prize, the Cavling Prize. Here are the stories from the last 9 years:

- 2009 Wrongdoings in the Ministry of Labour (DR P1)
- 2010 Wrongdoings against Danish military veterans (Jyllands-Posten)
- 2011 Wrongdoings against immigrants (Information)
- 2012 Wrongdoings against abused children (NORDJYSKE)
- 2013 Wrongdoings by companies in tax havens (DR)
- 2014 Wrongdoings by doctors (Jyllands-Posten)
- 2015 Wrongdoings against hostages in Syria (DR)
- 2016 Wrongdoings in the Ministry of Agriculture (Berlingske)

Truly great reporting done by great journalists. The point here is once more that this kind of reporting where journalists document problems and find the ones to blame, is mostly what the news culture rewards. And yes, my own Cavling Prize in 1990 was along the same lines – documenting wrongdoings in the mortgage industry.

Finally, let's think about the winners of The World Press Photo, the prize that any news photographer at any local or national daily dreams of winning. From looking at the winning pictures, news photographers all around the world know by heart where to point their cameras next time: At the hunger, at the wars, at the natural disasters, the victims, the refugees, the mothers in despair. Always fantastic photos, documenting the darkest sides of human life in the brightest colours. The point again is not that these are not great pictures and examples of prime journalism. The point is only this: This is the culture we have created.

When I was invited to talk for the newsroom at the Danish quality paper Kristeligt Dagblad (a national version of Christian Science

Monitor) I googled how often they write about their core beat, which one would think should be resurrection and joy: 57,703 hits. But it turned out that even Kristeligt Dagblad write far more about sorrow: 72,000 hits.

Moment of Truth

I remember my own moment of truth well. The exact time I found myself in front of the mirror, and didn't like what I saw.

It was a Friday evening in September 2008 after a long week at work. I had been in my job as head of DR News for more than a year, so I was responsible for the national news on radio, in TV and online at DR – one tenth the size of the BBC, but with 100 percent of its problems.

It should have been a great weekend. Everything was perfect: I was together with my beautiful wife and kids, I had a glass of red wine in my hand, a bowl of sweets on the coffee table and a film to watch on TV later. But first we had to watch the evening news on DR, just like any other decent family in the country to get the "best obtainable version of the truth" on life in Denmark and the rest of the world. It went like this:

Best obtainable version of the truth?

TV Avisen, DR's evening News 6.30 PM, Friday, September 8, 2018.

1. Welcome
2. **Terror threat** against Denmark
3. **Shooting** incident in Copenhagen
4. New regional trains not **delivered** on time
5. Cervical **cancer a danger** to young girls
6. **Strike** among bus drivers continue
7. Woman **abducted and abused**
8. **Crisis** in the Social Democratic Party
9. Old man runs for president in a US in **crisis**

10. Court case about airplane **accident** begins
11. **Suppressed** North Koreans work out
12. A giant mechanical spider creates **fear** in Liverpool
13. And the weather forecast: **The rain continues**.

I thought to myself, "Is the world really like that?" I went over all the stories again, and all of them fit our normal criteria for news. But was the big picture we presented to the Danish public in fact the best obtainable version of the truth – or just the result of our news culture?

And worse, if we presented that kind of picture of the world evening after evening, day after day, did we give an accurate picture or a completely false echo of reality? Had we then done our job to inform the Danes? And was I at all a good editor, working for the benefit of society?

Holder of the Microphone

The worst thing anyone can say to me or to any other journalist with any ambition is this: "You just hold the microphone." It means: "You are not critical enough in your interview and approach."

So, we compensate by being extra critical. Often to the extent where we are close to being aggressive using the microphone as a lance or the pen like a dagger.

In 2015, I did a talk for the newsroom at the public service company in Tallinn, Estonia. At some point a reporter in his 30s rose from his seat and said:

"I am sitting here getting a bit embarrassed. I cover business in Estonia. And I must admit that you are right, that I would really hate it if my colleagues, my editors or the competitors of the people I interview accused me of not being critical. So I mostly do stories about companies that are corrupt, fire people, pollute or are in bad shape financially."

"What's wrong with that?" I asked.

"Maybe I give my viewers a false picture of business in our country? Not that I tell lies. But I happen to think that I might get the picture wrong when I don't cover companies that are not corrupt, hire people and have stopped polluting. In fact, things have really improved, but I never do stories about that."

At a Danish university, a young journalism student raised her arm in frustration when I talked to her, her professors and her fellow future journalists.

"What you talk about is somewhat interesting. But it must be a lie, because, we learn that the goal of good journalism is to be critical. And that's not what you're saying, is it?" I replied, it was not, but that she had a great point:

The goal of great journalism is to tell important stories to people so that they can make up their own mind. To do that, you need to be critical. Ask tough questions, find out what he says is also what he does, keep power accountable. Being critical is not the goal in and of itself. It's the most important tool for a good reporter. But in news reporting, over the last 20-30 years, we have mixed up objectives and means without even noticing it.

Hypothesis Journalism

A very common working method at news organisations is to work with hypotheses: If the world was like this, it would be a really good story. It's much like the way good scientific researchers work. Only in science, you also publish results that contradict the hypothesis. In journalism, oftentimes the story is dropped if reality turns out to be different than what was expected.

Some, however, get bitten by the hypothesis bug, where the reporter and news organisation look only for information, sources and quotes, which can back the hypothesis, and they leave out any information that contradicts it or which would make the story more balanced with nuances. This one-eyed journalist sets off in quest of such facts that will substantiate his hypothesis whilst omitting to seek out the figures, tables or research results that will provide a more nuanced picture – or perhaps even undermine his hypothesis. Next, he will incorporate expert testimonies to make it look like real documentation. Preferably from someone who will be prepared to give know-all and citable statements. Then, all that is left to do is to contact a politician who will be more than willing to appear in the paper or on television, and then the story is complete. A story that will easily make good copy and which is not false. But is it true?

A Danish TV documentary on young girls claiming that they were getting ill from a new vaccine against cancer caused by human papilloma virus, HPV, had a great impact. Only 30 percent of young girls now say yes to the vaccine compared to 80 percent in our neighbouring countries. It was well produced, well told and scary. But was it made with the ambition to inform girls and their parents so they could make up their own mind, or was it made with the ambition to make a "good story" with high ratings and lots of attention? The problem with the so called "good story" is not that it told lies. But that it was all feelings and no evidence. Both the health authorities and the Danish Cancer Society have later criticised the documentary for creating fear for no reason:

"We have the first vaccine against cancer, but due to journalism thousands of girls increase their risk for no reason," director of the Danish Cancer Society, Leif Vestergaard, says regretfully.

Source: Global news headlines

No North Korean Version of News

Don't be mistaken: I love my profession and I do not want journalists to be boy scouts. In my mind, real journalists are indeed watchdogs. Independent, uncorrupt and always seeking the best obtainable version of the truth. We represent the most important profession in any democracy. Go to any country and see if the national press is allowed to report critically about the president without the risk of prison, death or other unpleasantness. If journalism is not free, democracy is dead.

I agreed then. And I agree today, more than 35 years later. But increasingly I am ashamed at how we as a media industry, publishing houses, newsrooms and as editors and reporters manage the power and the influence we have on society, on politics and our common future. What has happened?

A conversation in June 2010 serves one version of an answer. It took place one year before the death of Steve Jobs, co-founder of Apple, who in two decades had transformed the personal computer, the Walkman, the telephone, the music industry and the animation film business. Steve Jobs had agreed to talk to Rupert Murdoch on the problems facing the news business. Murdoch is the CEO of News Corp., the global giant of the media world with ownership of Sky News, Fox News, The Wall Street Journal, the New York Post, British newspapers The Times, The Sunday Times, and tabloid newspaper, The Sun. Murdoch wanted Jobs to have Apple's iTunes Store do for the print business what the digital platform had done for the music industry, creating a legal model to use for easily buying content in a digital world. According to Steve Jobs, who spoke about the conversation to the biographer Walter Isaacson, he told Murdoch that the problems for the news business were not only related to eroding financial models or a too slow transformation from an analogue to a digital age. It was about mindset, content and its role in society:

"The axis today is not liberal and conservative," Jobs explained his view on the change in news media to Murdoch during a dinner.

"The axis is constructive-destructive, and you've cast your lot with the destructive people. Fox has become an incredible destructive force in our society. You can be better, and this is going to be your legacy, if you are not careful."

One year later Murdoch was forced to shut down his British tabloid, The News of The World, following the scandal of the methods used by the paper, among them the routine of hacking the phones of celebrities. And therefore, the reputation of his company suffered.

How did it go so wrong, and was Jobs right in pointing to the news axis no longer being between different political directions and ideologies, but between the different roles they play in society? A choice between being constructive or destructive?

In my mind, traditional news journalism builds on four tendencies in society that merged into the newsrooms in the 1970s.

- The first was a commercialisation of news where tabloid media in the late 60s and early 70s became successful with their different approach to journalism than the so-called serious media for the elites: Tabloid media wanted to entertain a broader audience with a preference for crime, scandals, sex, celebrities and sports. It focused on the little man against the system, simplified issues and turned political coverage into matters of individual people rather than visions and ideology. This approach quickly spilled over into local TV news and from there, into mainstream media.
- The second was the anti-authority riot of the 1968 movement which attracted many politically motivated activists to journalism, seeing news media as an important tool to put social injustice on the public agenda and keep the political establishment accountable.
- The third important trend to form newsroom culture in recent decades originates from the Watergate scandal uncovered by the Washington Post and the publication of the Pentagon papers by The New York Times. Both stories were seen by new generations of journalists as proof of both the power of the free press and how political power could not be trusted. It created new heroes and defined truly great reporting.

- The fourth is a massive investment in PR and communication in interest groups, industry and political parties: They all know that perception is reality, and they use every means to make the public see the world through their eyes. They also know that media coverage is both cheaper and more credible to the population and try to influence the stories covered by news media. They are extremely effective in serving the right problems, the right victims, the catchy conflict and the drama which tricks all the boxes of the traditional instincts of most news organisations.

Now the question is, where have these four trends taken journalism, news media and the public debate?

Bad News

In many Western countries, the press is in fact better than its reputation. A great deal of good journalism helps people get updated, become more knowledgeable, and helps them make up their own minds. And yet still I claim that far too much news reporting has become one-eyed, negative, and trivial.

In a 1997 study about attitudes towards the press by the American nonprofit research group, Public Agenda, it was found that 79 percent of respondents agreed with the statement: "A reporter's job is to cover bad news."

In the United States, where competition for attention and ad revenue in local markets in all the big cities is intense, TV crews compete to get to the scene before ambulance crews and frame all political stories in terms of politicians' attacks on their opponents. In the spring of 2011, I visited a local TV station in the Los Angeles area which had about twice the ratings of Denmark's leading public service channel DR1, and I saw that the channel had subdivided the newsroom into four broad categories: Crime, traffic, weather and scandals. 'Scandals' was the name of the desk where the so-called political reporters worked. This was the channel that kept local residents informed of local politics and the challenges facing Los Angeles, the United States and the world. What sort of worldview are their viewers likely to end up with?

If it Bleeds, it Leads

'If it bleeds, it leads' is the cynical slogan typical of the editorial standpoint across American local news media that promotes the myth that to be successful, mass media communications need an unhealthy dose of blood and guts. American media take this axiom seriously and are full of sensationalist attempts to out-shout the opposition with headlines like 'Plastic surgery disasters' 'Killer bras?', 'Can frozen yogurt make you ill?' or the jewel in the crown, 'What's happening in our public toilets?', which TV news channel, Channel 13 News, used in New Mexico a few years ago to scare parents into believing that paedophiles were using 50 of the state's public toilets as a base for their activities. Backed by dramatic music and with a rifle sight as a logo, a deep voice promised that Channel 13 would investigate. The report later revealed that journalists had investigated three toilets and found nothing. The entire series, which ran for several evenings, was based on a police report of two possible incidents at the same location during which a man had taken off his clothes.

This might be just an example of terrible journalism of course, but perhaps it is also an example of the stories we as a profession look to because we believe it's the only way to generate attention, ratings, views and advertising revenue/legitimacy for the licence fee.

As the vice chairman for the Committee of Concerned Journalists, and now executive director for The American Press Institute, Tom Rosenstiel wrote in a report on American local TV news: "Newsroom decision makers operate by a set of elaborate, long-held assumptions about what motivates viewers, reinforced by anecdote, inference and corporate mandate."

He has data to back his critique on American news journalism: Almost two thirds of the 33,000 news stories at 154 local TV stations all over the United States opened on crime, accidents or a disaster. In the book 'We Interrupt This Newscast' from 2007, Rosenstiel and his research team show that 73 percent of stories about politics are less than a minute long, and more than a third are less than 30 seconds.

"Local TV news is the main source of information for many Americans about what is happening in their neighbourhood, their economy and their culture. How well news serves its audience matters not only for the station's bottom line but also for the bottom line of the democratic enterprise," Rosenstiel warns, and serves one explanation to those who find that the general American public has little knowledge about the outside world.

"The assumptions in the newsroom management ... are reinforced by limited resources, lack of time, lack of reporter expertise, and growing demand for more programming – all conditions that are on the increase ... But many of the current newsroom conventions lead to the practices that annoy not only critics of TV news but also viewers as well."

American doctor and lecturer at New York University School of Medicine, Marc Siegel, knows the exact meaning of that statement. Siegel has written an interesting book entitled False Alarm, and in it he attacks the industries that make a living out of frightening people unnecessarily. His critique isn't limited to the pharmaceuticals industry (which he criticises for influencing medical practice in the West in the direction of managing illness rather than curing it), the media is also the subject of his ire:

"Fear invades our homes as never before, and it is affecting growing numbers of people. Newspaper headlines are apocalyptic warnings. The media's obsession with fear pours fuel on our worries, which burn out only to be replaced by further alarming news items."

Negativity is an illness

Roland Schatz agrees. He is the founder and CEO of Media Tenor, a Swiss-based international company doing analysis on media content all over the world for governments, interest groups, media companies and other businesses with offices in Europe, Russia, the United States,

Vietnam, South Africa and Australia. His message is not popular in newsrooms:

"Negativity is an illness caught by even serious newspapers, magazines and not least TV news broadcasters all over the Western world. Our surveys show that up to 60 percent of all news stories deal with problems and things that are wrong, depending on the country and the media. The problem is that the world is not like that, but news organisations feverously go on painting a far too dark picture of reality."

Schatz, who has shared his research in newsrooms and universities on all continents, underlines that the press does not lie directly:

"The problem is not that their numbers are wrong. The problem is that the picture is wrong, because most news reporters systematically ignore the facts which do not fit into the traditional negative news angle. Reporters tell for instance that the big German companies fire people, but they ignore that small and family-owned German companies, at the same time, hire more people than the big ones lay off. The public and the elected leaders get the wrong impression that the German unemployment rate is going up, when in fact, it is going down. This journalistic negativity sickness creates fear and ignorance; it is bad for the press itself, bad for people, bad for politics, bad for business and bad for the future. I consider this one of the most dangerous tendencies in our democracies."

World's Best News

In Denmark, the frustration of the traditional news media has led to a very untraditional initiative called the World's Best News. Supported by the Government, NGOs and the United Nations, it aims to circumvent the traditional news media's focus on suffering, and to change Danes' attitudes. The most interesting is not the message itself, but the distribution channels. Instead of trying to persuade news media to tell the facts or run costly ads, the organisers chose to use milk cartons, apples and bread bags to get their message out:

"More than ever before, it's important to provide a platform for success stories. How many people know, for example, that 1.8 billion people have gained access to clean water in recent years," he says Thomas Ravn-Pedersen, head of the World's Best News, where I have had a seat on the board since 2016.

"The newest UN figures show that even though there are significant challenges ahead, the efforts we have made so far have created significant and lasting improvements in the living conditions of hundreds of millions of people in developing countries. The clear majority of children in developing countries now receive an education, and fewer die of malaria," Ravn-Pedersen says.

"We want to tell that story, and it has turned out to be too difficult to get traditional media to tell it for us. So, we have found other ways that are just as effective to tell the facts of the world." The World's Best News tells stories like:

- 17,000 fewer children now die every day than in 1990.
- 90 percent of the world's population now have access to clean drinking water.
- Deforestation of wood has dropped 3.1 million acres per year
- Since 2000 the number of people who die from malaria is down by 42 percent.

Journalistic Cynicism

The fact that it is necessary to use milk cartons and not newsprint or broadcasting to get the facts straight, does not surprise a growing number of people in public office who express a growing frustration towards what they see as a tabloidisation of news. This frustration is evident when one listens to the former speaker of the Danish Parliament, Mogens Lykketoft, who served as president of the United Nations General Assembly in 2016:

"It endangers democracy when news media, in order to let sensationalism attract a larger audience, in reality becomes the least responsible of the four pillars of power in society .... As a public, we do not get any smarter or wiser. And society does not improve."

In a keynote at the global broadcast conference NewsXchange in Marrakesh in November 2013, CNN's skilled reporter Christiane Amanpour raised a warning flag to our profession:

"We need to keep thinking about what it is that we do and how we want to be relevant every day ... We need to find a balance between holding government and all those in authority accountable without flipping to the other side and creating a cynicism based on a false premise, that all governments, all authorities, all elected are somehow corrupt, war criminals and all the rest. By doing so, we risk undermining further civil society by adding to the public notion that every form of authority is useless, hopeless and doesn't work."

Her worry of a growing journalistic cynicism finds support in the results of a study published by The Associated Press in 2008. It found that young consumers of news felt 'debilitated by information overload and unsatisfying news experiences': Adding to news fatigue among these participants was the widespread belief that all news today is negative, the report noted. Repeatedly in the study, the negativity of news (tragedy, crisis, war, terror) added to the desire to tune out.

A survey amongst Danes, made by Analyse Denmark for DR in December 2011, supports the public dissatisfaction of traditional news:

- 75 percent of viewers said that they are tired of watching politicians quarrel on TV;
- 50 percent said that news programs focus too much on conflicts;
- 5 percent wanted more stories on conflicts;
- 83 percent asked for more stories inspiring solutions to the challenges facing society and the world.

And tune out they do. Young readers and viewers leave traditional news media in the millions or even worse, they never tune in. Instead they turn to other media sources, with one of the most popular being social media like Facebook where they can concentrate on their own interest, their own friends, their own self-image and be less inclined to be confronted with conflicting views of the world besides their own.

Irrelevant Content

Erik Rasmussen is the CEO of the international Danish think tank Sustania. He is former editor-in-chief of several quality news magazines and business papers and a frequent participant at The World Economic Forum meetings in Davos. His critique of traditional news media sounds ruthless:

"If the media, especially the news organisations, believe to have a responsibility for democracy and being one of its main pillars, it is now they have to prove it by revitalising their own role. If not, they undermine their own importance and risk a justified critique for weakening, and not strengthening, democracy. We see newspapers all over the Western world losing circulation and trying to cut costs, but the reason is not only competition from new digital media. The main reason is that traditional news organisations have not in due time redefined their task and responsibility. Just like it is not a strategy to go on cutting costs, the future is not a new financial model on the web. The solution is a serious shift in focus. The problem is not the media itself or the change of distribution of news. The problem is when the content becomes useless." And Erik Rasmussen does not stop there:

"Most news media now follow a strategy of a journalism focusing on processes and people and covering conflicts and crises in combination with a widespread use of commentators and opinion polls in an effort to set new agendas. The ambition seems to be clear in every newsroom: To be the first to trigger the next political scandal and/or topple a minister or even better, the whole government. Nothing indicates that this strategy will save the media. On the contrary, it risks locking journalists in a position among the least trustworthy in society."

Imagine

The customary view of traditional journalism would be to stop at documenting just another problem and then asking the responsible minister or CEO for a response. He would then blame his predecessors, call for more money or more control. Another more and more popular strategy is to blame the media, which only leads to editors and publishers shooting back at the politicians, accusing them of interfering with the free and independent press.

Just imagine if we in the press began with ourselves, dared to look in the mirror and start changing the things we do not like. Imagine if we had the guts to get involved in a dialogue on how we could improve together. Imagine if we spent less effort on shooting at each other, disagreeing and fighting over who is to blame. Imagine if we could inspire each other to find new roads for journalism, for media, for politics, for society, and for the future.

Perhaps the time has come where we in the press should be just as critical towards ourselves and assess our own bad habits that we are always seeing in everybody else? I think it has.

Imagine if we agreed on the fact that good journalism can also be inspirational and provide good stories about possible solutions. Stories that show that the world is not only crazy, evil and dangerous, but that it is also full of options, hope, joy and people who dare do new stuff, dreaming of a better tomorrow.

Imagine if we dared to supplement the traditional news criteria with a new one: Constructive news. As Albert Einstein once said: "Without changing our pattern of thought, we will not be able to solve the problems we created with our current pattern of thought."

The time has come to form a rebellion against the tabloidisation of news. It is time to get out of the strait jacket that the tabloids have put on even the so-called serious media. The focus of the yellow press on dallying entertainment, postulating drama, simplistic conflicts, haunt on everybody with power, and the claim to be the true defender against the evil system has for years been the key to success in the media industry.

Also for the so-called serious media in their struggle against boredom, routine and their elitist humanity talking down to or over the heads of the masses, it turns out that the public found alternatives in the tabloids and magazines. These media follow their mission to help people kill time, which also became the concept for TV news: Make it short, make it uncomplicated, make it fast, make it dramatic and undifferentiated, so that the conflict is clear.

The concept is evident when a person running for office comes up with a new idea He gets dragged into a TV studio opposite his worst political opponent, who clearly starts by telling the interviewer and the audience why this is the most ridiculous idea he's ever heard, and proceeds to attack his opponent's intellect, trustworthiness or morals. Can the interviewer turn the fight physical? After all, it is good television. A little verbal boxing for one minute and 40 seconds will do, before the anchor routinely interrupts with 'I guess you won't agree tonight, we have run out of time, but the debate continues. Thank you both for being with us tonight'.

Who got any wiser? What was the new idea? Was it any good? Where do they agree? Where is the solution to the problem that the public really wants to have fixed?

The two politicians forget those questions as they withdraw from the TV spotlight to each of their ring corners. Here they meet their growing army of PR agents, spin doctors and one-liner writers who immediately continue to train them to get more airtime by attacking faster, sounding smarter and communicating directly into the real news criteria of traditional media:

Do you know them by now?

Conflict, drama, victims and villains.

Chapter 3

WHY WE NEED TO CHANGE

*Too strong a media emphasis on death and violence
can lead to despair.*

Dalai Lama, Spiritual leader

The professor still remembers when he realised that journalists suffer from a collective disease. He had a call from a reporter who had been told by her editor to try to do more exciting stories on something which works well, instead of the normal focus on only the misery in society.

"Try out this new constructive journalism thing," the editor had said.

The journalist was responsible for a program on national TV and needed help. Hans Henrik Knoop, an assistant professor of psychology at the Aarhus University in Denmark, was happy when he was asked if media negativity affected people. Knoop, who also served as chairman of The European Network for Positive Psychology, told the reporter of the vast research showing that the subject was both important and urgent. He also offered to participate on TV and talk about the importance of inspiration and hope, even when reporting on death and destruction.

However, the journalist wasn't interested. All she looked for was a psychologist who had treated patients who had collapsed due to media negativity. Smiling knowingly, Professor Knoop reflects: "Even the most evident possibility to tell an inspirational story had to be negatively angled to fit the traditional journalistic template."

But Knoop's research does show that negative focus influences the mental condition of a nation: "News media is now so full of stories on misery. Negativity controls news flow, and therefore also politics and public debate. And it has consequences: In the same way as you know that you become what you eat, you psychologically become what you focus on. You can eat a lot without getting proper nutrition, just as you can use your attention in ways that only leave you with a sense of emptiness. Empty calories in the food make us rapidly slower, fatter and more tired, and the same thing goes for a superficial public debate. Rapidly people turn mentally fat. If they only hear about piles of problems and people who disagree and argue disrespectfully, they mentally turn off. Apathy or fear is the result. The risk is that people not only deselect media as sources for news, but also that they disengage in the public debate due to the extreme priority of the negative".

Knoop explains the biological reason why the negative focus is so powerful: "10,000 years ago, human life was poor, nasty, brutish and short. Daily life in the stone age was full of threats of hunger, thirst, enemies, wild animals and deadly diseases. Therefore, the human brain is genetically trained to being alert at all times, and that's why negative stories are so much more powerful than positive stories. Three times more powerful at work, and five times more powerful in your marriage."

Perhaps this could be the reason why it takes several *I love you*'s to neutralise one single honest answer to your wife's question "Does my bum look big in this?" Knoop further argues that negative reporting disengages, whereas constructive angles engage:

"If we want engaged citizens, who fight to solve the small and big problems of the world, who believe they can make a difference, then media have to do their part of the work. When politicians argue on TV, they accuse each other of lying, deliberately remembering things wrong, of double standards, of breach of promise, of cheating, using false figures and of hidden agendas – it is disengaging. In normal life, a friendship would never survive minutes of that kind of communication, at work or in a marriage, even less. Journalists are to a large degree responsible for the fundamental distrust the public has towards politicians. Of course journalists have to be watchdogs, but nobody has said that their job is to create their own villains."

In the eyes of psychologists, the scary truth is that we in the media not only cover the local and global conflicts, we also prolong them too. The logic of any conflict is that what each party does to defend themselves, the other party uses as an argument for continuing the battle. And the news media are happy spectators and participants: we report on the one-sided and provocative statements from each side. In this way, we not only report on the conflicts. We keep them alive and make them grow.

Consequences for Political Leadership

All across Europe, it is getting increasingly difficult to attract suitable applicants for public office. Former Danish parliamentary speaker, Mogens Lykketoft, finds the quality of candidates for political office to be a subject of serious concern, and, in his opinion, the blame lies firmly with the media. He recalls an article in the Danish Tabloid, Ekstra Bladet, in which the contents of a garbage can from the private home of a minister was published:

"When the media cast every aspect of your private life in the most unfortunate light possible, of course politicians have to consider whether it's really something they want to put themselves through. It's not that well paid."

Now we are getting to the heart of the issues which worry the vast majority of party leaders, but which they are reluctant to comment on publicly because it would involve hard-hitting criticism of their party colleagues. Lykketoft mentions what a party leader said to him during an unguarded moment:

"Several the most talented young members of our party never go in for national politics. It's just too unrewarding. The problem is that the ones who do, don't always do so for the right reasons."

Similarly, a parliamentary group leader told me about a meeting he held with a couple of members of his party's youth wing who were keen to get his advice about how best to get into parliament:

"I heard myself say, don't bother, it's not worth it. I hate the fact that I said it, but I did. That's just the way it is. Politics has just become too unrewarding. And of course, it's not just the media's fault, but they certainly share the blame."

During my childhood, my parents had a neighbour who was offered a parliamentary constituency by a group of respectable local citizens. This was something they were proud of. A parliamentary candidate, indeed a Member of Parliament, you could hardly get a more prestigious job than that. Today, tales of constituencies searching desperately for candidates are commonplace. And when someone does finally stand, people usually assume that they're doing so because they couldn't get a proper job.

Jørn Henrik Pedersen, professor of political science at the University of Southern Denmark, has spent his life conducting research on Danish politics; he has also worked in media as the former Chairman of publicly owned TV station TV2, is the founder of the School of Journalism at the University of Southern Denmark, and has been the chairman of a regional media group, Fynske Medier. "A sort of death spiral has set in between media and politicians, which means that both groups are accorded less and less respect. I have very little respect for opinion polls, but even so, it's striking that journalists and politicians always end up at the bottom of trustworthiness indices."

For many years, the Danish politician Jens Rohde was a well-known so-called "whip" for his party, Denmark's Liberal Party (Venstre). He is now elected to his second term in the European Parliament for the Danish Social Liberal Party (Det Radikale Venstre), and in October 2014 he publicly gave his 6 pieces of advice to younger and less experienced politicians on how to be successful in a political debate in the national parliament. According to the Danish tabloid BT they go like this:

1. Speak in a way so people can feel you. Invest in yourself. It is okay to be entertaining.
2. Give short answers and then attack. The longer you answer a question the more you expose yourself and are forced into the defensive. So answer very briefly and then attack.

3. When you know all the corners of the policy of your own party, focus on the policy of the political program of your opponents. Only in this way you can find their weak spots.
4. Ask open questions. It forces your opponent to expose himself, and then you hit him. Ask him to repeat, what he has just said. It is evil, but it works. The less experienced politician will freeze.
5. Never give people nick names. Doing that shows that you are in the defensive.
6. Make sure that your colleagues from your own party act like a wolf pack and concentrate on one issue. Do not give the opponent the chance to get off the hook.

That political culture has its prize: The popular Social Democratic mayor of Aarhus Jacob Bundsgaard, educated in political science, would be a normal candidate for government as were three mayors from Denmarks 2nd biggest city before him. But he has made his choice:

"I don't want to join national politics. I cannot see myself getting up every morning with the purpose of undermining the credibility of my opponents in the media." The similarly successful mayor of the Danish city Herning, Lars Krarup, has also turned down several offers to become a minister for his party, Denmark's Liberal Party.

"I don't want my children to see me being chased by the press all the time. It's just not worth it."

What do we expect?

Niels Krause-Kjær, political analyst and now news anchor at DR, commented on his blog (hosted by Danish news site berlingske.dk) in 2012 about the depths plumbed by political journalism:

"It's time to reflect a bit about how far all of us – citizens, bloggers, op-ed writers, journalists and politicians are willing to go to debase politics and politicians. Isn't it about time we showed a bit more respect and common sense? What do we expect? That the country's Prime Minister should come out and scrub the pavement clean every hour on the hour so we can all watch, because we don't find it ok to spend taxpayers' money on a smoker's cabin in the Prime Minister's office? It's a small step from that to the tabloid press' exaggerated horror at the fact that Danish Prime Minister, Helle Thorning-Schmidt's new desk cost all of 39,000 Danish Kroner. Again, I ask, what do we expect? That the prime minister should welcome the German Chancellor or the French President with Ikea furniture?"

Danish businessman, Asger Aamund, who has been suggested to run for public office for several political parties, understands the difficulty in recruiting talented individuals to political office:

"There's too little prestige. Wages aren't competitive. The opportunity to exert influence is slight, and the personal costs are far too big. With the result that many people who would otherwise have been attracted to political office, take their talents elsewhere. This lack of leadership ability amongst Danish politicians is one of the greatest challenges facing Danish democracy."

But politicians want to be re-elected, which is why they spend more and more of their time trying to cast themselves in terms of the media's newsworthiness criteria: drama, conflicts, victims, and villains. As a prominent member of the Danish Parliament explained to me in desperation a couple of years ago:

"We can't get airtime anymore unless we're prepared to attack someone. And we use so much money and spend so much time at perfecting the art that we end up forgetting what it is we want to do. What sort of politics we actually stand for. There simply aren't any journalists who are interested in hearing about that."

In a public debate on the myths of teenagers and alcohol in the summer of 2017 at the political Festival Folkemødet, a question from the audience produced a surprisingly honest answer.

The Social Democratic member of parliament, Tine Bramsen, was asked why she criticised the government in the news media for not doing enough to prevent teenagers aged 13 and 14 from drinking alcohol.

"New statistics show that 94 percent of the children in 8th grade have never even so much as tasted alcohol. And that is a massive improvement compared the recent years. Why didn't you mention that?" the voter asked.

"I would not have been quoted in the news if I hadn't criticised that 6 percent of children in 8th grade have tasted alcohol," Bramsen stated, acknowledging that the result was just one more story in the news leaving the public with the false picture that Danish teenagers drink more and more.

For years, politicians in many western countries such as the United States, France, Spain, Denmark and not least Greece, birthplace of democracy, have raised the national debt, because they were afraid of what would happen to their own political future if they made unpopular cuts on public spending that would hit large voting groups. However, as soon as a member of parliament, a minister or a government was daring enough to propose changes, then the story was instinctively covered according to the prevailing tabloid news criteria:

- The conflict angle: Who is opposed to these measures? Aren't they at odds with the party's former line?
- The drama angle: What do the opinion polls say? Are the party's members happy with the proposals? Will they lose their seats at the next election?
- The victim angle: What do pensioner organisations have to say (they oppose ...)? Can we drum up a dentist who feels disappointed and angry at the prospect of not being able to retire at the age he or she has been looking forward to retiring for years? Or can we find someone with a manual labor job whose working life has been so demanding that it would be hard on them to continue to work into old age?
- The villain angle: What on earth does the MP/Minister think he or she is playing at? They're in breach of their promise.

A few years ago, the former Danish Minister of Health, Bertel Haarder, agreed to the obligatory interview after a documentary had revealed that some tattoo parlours had been tattooing people under the legal age limit. He was asked the inevitable question: "What are you going to do about it?"

"Okay," said the minster, "I'll introduce more controls then, but don't come back to me afterwards with some story about how the government has tied everything up in red tape." There spoke the voice of experience.

As only a former minister with a lifetime's experience as an elected representative can put it: "It's a democratic problem that the media's management, who are not popularly elected, exercise such a degree of influence over the political agenda. It's the media's eternal focus on victims and the need for greater public-sector provision that has contributed to the perceived need for even greater public sector expenditure. If there was the same focus on excess spending as there is on the lack of it, the world would be a very different place."

Scarce Resources

News and information are no longer elements that modern individuals lack. The truth is rather that they are drowning in them. Modern man already has too much information, news, products, channels, opportunities and technologies. It's no surprise that traditional media is in a state of crisis, and that there are almost no media organisations anywhere on the planet that can put together a sustainable business model that is built on selling standard news, whether in print or on the Internet. It's a basic economic question of the relation between supply and demand – when there's too much of a product, the price falls, and falls until it eventually hits zero.

Futurist Anne Skare Nielsen from the Danish company, Future Navigator, has made an alternative list of the things that modern people will lack in the future: Originality, intimacy, care, consideration, trust and time.

What does this mean? This means that in the future, smart media will try to deliver the things that people lack, instead of putting all their efforts into products people can get anywhere and may even be able to get far cheaper and quicker elsewhere.

- Originality – let's make it unique.
- Intimacy – let's make it up close, whether in a geographical or emotional sense.
- Care – let's make our stories take care of people and society.
- Consideration – let's make our stories provide understanding, knowledge and perspective.
- Trust – let's be authoritative and believable.
- Time – let's help others make decisions. Let's prioritise and focus on people's need and not think our job is to give them more, but to clean up the mess.

As more and more news people realise: This all applies to constructive journalism.

PART 2

INSPIRATION FOR A SOLUTION

Chapter 4

A GOOD STORY

I believe that good journalism, good television,
can make the world a better place.

Christiane Amanpour, CNN correspondent

One story from DR News showed me that we had to change. Not because we ran it. But because we didn't.

As the new head of news at DR back in 2007, I was increasingly puzzled with the culture and traditions in Danish newsrooms, and I started to talk to my new colleagues about our work and editorial habits. One of the experienced reporters recalled finding some statistics a couple of years earlier which detailed employment rates amongst female immigrants by municipal authority. It didn't look good.

Unemployment among immigrant women was greater than average in every single town and city in Denmark, with one exception: 0 percent unemployment among female immigrants in the Danish municipality of Fredericia. The journalist was so surprised that he contacted the city hall to ask whether their data had been entered correctly.

"Oh yes, it's quite true," they explained. "It's the Lene effect."

"The what?"

"Well, you see a couple of years ago we got a new immigrant consultant called Lene. And she just gets on well with these women. She's won their trust, and she started to take them out to meetings at companies all over town. She booked herself a meeting with the CEO, kicked the door in and said:

"This is Fatima, she's fantastic. She can help you do something you need doing. What it is, we don't know yet. That's what this meeting is all about. And what's the worst thing that can happen? If I'm wrong, it won't cost you a dime as her wages will be paid by the government for the first three months. Now come on, give her a chance."

Within 18 months all the women were employed. The reporter enthusiastically called the then TV News Editor with his story about the Lene effect.

"That's not a story," was the response. "Where's the conflict in that? Why should we give airtime to a commercial for the mayor running that city?" And so the Lene effect story never ran.

That would come as no surprise for Syrian-born Danish politician Naser Khader, who started his own party, only to leave politics again to work for an American think tank in Washington D.C.

Naser Khader is now re-elected to parliament for The Conservative People's Party (Det Konservative Folkeparti). In 2011, with the help of friends, he organised a conference at the parliament in Copenhagen with more than 100 examples of entrepreneurial immigrants who had started their own business and created jobs. He describes his experience:

"I wanted to show that there is another side of the stereotypical picture of poor, passive or fanatic immigrants we see in the media. We invited all the newspapers, radio stations and TV shows. We sent out press releases, we called them and had the most fantastic people lined up. Do you know how many reporters or photographers came? Not one! Can you imagine the media turnout, if instead we had arranged a conference on the fanatic Muslims group Hizb ut-Tahrir? There are not so many of them as there are immigrant entrepreneurs, but the rest of the population learns only about the fanatics, because that is the story news organisations want to run."

What's New?

Hearing about a neighbours' annual holiday in Mallorca is normally extremely boring:

"First we drove to the airport, and then we took the plane to Palma and drove in the sunshine to the hotel we always visit. And then we spent eight days relaxing by the pool ..." They are usually not even halfway through their story before we start yawning.

But are we only interested if their story turns out to deal with them forgetting their passports? Or even better, if they forgot the little brother in the airport, their baggage ended up in Kazakhstan, and it snowed on the beach? Wouldn't we also be keen to learn, that they got a great deal with their hotel, found a smaller airport with free parking, explored a new facility teaching kids the language during the sailing classes, and learning about the new rules, such as how to make airlines pay money back when they run late or even cancel flights? That's why news stories are seldom about normality. A news item is precisely the opposite – a deviation from the norm. So, when most things work fine, the logic is that news is about things that do not. But who told us that deviation from the norm is only of interest, when it's negative?

The problem first arises when we see the world only through negative eyes, when our vision is distorted. As Danish author and history lecturer, Henrik Jensen, puts it in his book The Dissent Man:

"We – or more properly our media – love people who break established norms and go over the limit. The aggressive victim who has been beaten down once more by the system. The charming crook. The drug dealer who commits murder, and ends up holding talks about it. The second-generation immigrant who went off the rails and became a gangster. Plus all the people with unusual diagnoses, the mentally ill, transsexuals, the overweight and the underweight."

The challenge that every journalist faces is that we know that the man has got a point. When our television, radio and newspapers are constantly braying that bus companies all over the country are losing both money and passengers and have cut their services back as a result and put their prices up, that becomes the norm. And as news is defined by something out of the ordinary, it is actually news, if you can find just one bus service in the nation that runs on time with satisfied customers and even makes money.

Danish broadcaster DR News found one. It was called Bus 150S and it run from Kokkedal north of Copenhagen. And we could do a fantastic report about all the many satisfied customers that used the route because the bus now ran on time, had free wi-fi and a driver who had learned to smile, clean the bus and to be proud of his job: "I say welcome to my bus!"

It is now proven that it can be done. So, if they can do it, why can't you?

The New DR

That approach is the direct result of a change in strategy for DR. Until 1988, DR held a monopoly on the TV market in Denmark and no one else was allowed to broadcast TV or radio other than the state owned, licensed and financed Danish Radio Company. A new commercial (but also state-owned) station, TV2, broke the monopoly on 1st October 1988 – a date that older DR employees often refer to as 'the day the good old days ended'.

It might have been good times for the employees with zero competition, but few Danes turned out to prefer the rather dull, slow and grey picture of the world presented on the state-owned, monopoly TV. In less than six years, DR lost 60 percent of its viewers to a faster and more modern competitor. For decades since, DR tried to come back by copying what its commercial competitor did, but with little success. As the market for TV changed with many new commercially and internationally owned players, everybody was competing for advertising money, with TV2 being more and more tabloid-like. DR had tried to follow by covering more crime stories, more royalty, more case-driven news stories and cutting down on coverage of complicated subjects such as the European Union and the economy, in an effort to attract more viewers. The tabloid strategy of more drama, more conflict, and the focus of narrow angles on crooks and people to feel sorry for, did not work. Viewership declined even more. A new management team and a new board decided on a different approach and began to ask the simple questions: What is the meaning of DR? Why are we here?

The answer was expressed in a new mission: DR shall inform, challenge and bring together people in Denmark. In short, everything that DR does has to be for the benefit of society. If the children's programs are not better to watch for Danish children than those being broadcasted on Fox Kids or the Disney Channel, then why should DR be here? If the drama series such as The Killing and Borgen are not of a higher quality for the Danish audience than cheaper TV series from the international electronic bulk market, why bother? And if the news programs now have a higher ambition to entertain, who will then take on the task of informing the many of important matters?

"We are here to throw light. Not to spread darkness and fear," said the Chairman of the DR board and the former CEO of The National Royal Theatre, Michael Christiansen. He continued:

"Knowledge and insights are the roads to tolerance, and tolerance is the key to a true democracy. It is said that media is in a crisis. I believe that the survival of serious media among other things is founded on a systematic and reinforced belief in the people we are here for."

In 2012, DR cut down on administration and invested more in quality content, like our news programs, with the ambition of re-establishing DR News as an authority being 'skilled in what we tell, modern in the way we tell it'. We cut down on the coverage of crime, entertainment and stories that were only fascinating. Instead we invested in more skilled reporters on beats like globalisation, business, politics and health. We opened new foreign bureaus and even though we moved our main news show on the main channel, DR1, from 9 p.m. to 9:30 p.m. and insisted on keeping our news hour filled with daily background magazines on international issues, money and politics, a strange thing happened: Viewers came back.

One of the reasons was that at the same time, we added constructive elements as natural stories in our daily broadcast. Every day, we wanted to have at least one story which could inspire by focusing on the things that work or the people, companies or countries who do something out of the ordinary. Let me give you a few examples:

- The story about a supermarket that employs autistic people as shelf stackers.
- The story about IKEA having started employing older craftsmen, because customers would rather be served by a man with grey hair

who knows how to hold a hammer, than a 19-year-old whose only experience in life is PlayStation games.

- The report on the municipality that uses money to train pensioners to manage their own lives rather than sending home helps out to them.
- The cardiologist who saved his own father's life with an invention that has gone on to be a huge export success.
- The municipality that has reduced sick leave rates by giving a bonus to staff that don't report in sick.
- The extensive decline in the number of burglaries as a result, in part, of an initiative taken by the police to send text messages to local residents when criminals have been sighted in the area.
- The care home with a play area that attracts kids from the nearby kindergarten.
- The boom in cycling in Athens, because due to the financial crisis, people have found healthier and cheaper transportation.
- The Mexican city which successfully fights the local drug gangs.
- The successful German idea: A hospice for dying children, who can spend their last months with their family with nurses and personnel trained to help, instead of dying at crowded hospitals or at home.
- And the story from Uganda, where a Danish electricity company has started to hand out solar lamps to replace polluting oil lamps.

That is what the concept of constructive news is all about: Giving the editorial glasses a polish so that we also see the stories about things that work. Things that dare to inspire to be both critical and constructive, to speak out about problems and actively search out stories that can contribute to a solution. Constructive news is all about daring to adjust our understanding of ourselves as journalists, so that we don't just see our task as a notice board for the public's problems and fears. Rather to ensure that we, to serve our society and the citizens it consists of, are also happy to take on a more active role as a sort of arbitrator in the public debate about the solutions to the challenges we all face.

Best Practice

Examples like these slowly changed the news culture at DR. And it is no longer only the editor-in-chief who asks for constructive angles on daily news meetings. At one of DR's editorial meetings, a talented reporter wanted to run a story based on new figures that showed that 61 percent of Danes think that they have their dream job. She was just about to put a negative angle on the story: That four out of ten want a new job – because that's the way we normally present things like that. However, she caught herself in the act and cautiously asked her colleagues whether it wouldn't be more interesting and more surprising, given the number of articles you can find about stress, burnouts and terrible managers to report to, that despite this, 60 percent of us can't actually imagine a better job than the one we have? She changed the angle on that story.

Another example is a survey sent to the nation's newsrooms, financed by the Danish Nurses' Organization, intended to spark debate about nurses' working conditions and their stress and wage levels. At DR, we took the view that this was not really news. We have all heard this story a thousand times before. Instead, our reporters tried to find an example of a hospital where management and nurses had done something about the problem, giving nurses a better working environment.

The result turned out to be great story. We found a hospital department just outside of Copenhagen where they had taken on two immigrant women as 'house assistants'. Their job was to help the nurses do their jobs. The house assistants made sure that stores were kept full, they dispatched journals, and poured patients' juice. The patients were happy because service levels improved, nurses were happy because they were no longer stressed, and management was happy because sick leave rates had fallen drastically, so much so that the financial savings covered the two women's salaries. The women were also happy because they were learning Danish and they smiled to the camera and said they thought Denmark was a great place to live.

There was no conflict and no drama, there were no victims and no villains. But it was news.

The next example was also newsworthy, and neither DR's viewers nor the chairperson of Local Government Denmark's healthcare committee will forget the day she was interviewed by a TV news team. The story's focus was on the increasing number of elderly patients who are left in hospitals even though their treatment has run its course. Municipalities don't do enough to get them home again.

The chairperson was ready to give the standard response that it was someone else's fault, for instance the government's or the hospital's fault. But then we showed a clip from a municipality that had actually taken steps to do something about the problem, and through targeted measures had both saved money and improved the lives of their elderly residents by helping them to return to their homes following their hospital stay. "Why don't you do that?" asked the newscaster in a friendly but firm tone. She suddenly looked like a fish out of water. That was critical constructive journalism at its best.

Denmark on the Brink

At DR, we decided to not merely talk about our habits – we wanted to change them. In 2010, we directed our focus to life outside the big cities and growth centres, and decided not to just focus on the problems.

We began by collecting a large amount of data relevant to the problems caused by the constant stream of unskilled jobs being outsourced to China or India – at the same time as public-sector restructuring meant that police officers, judges, soldiers and doctors were moving to population centres. We also systematically looked for stories that could present a potential solution to these problems.

Correspondents in America travelled to Detroit to see how entire districts are being torn down instead of leaving dilapidated housing as a frightful reminder of what had gone before. DR's journalists found two Danish villages just kilometers away from each other, where the varying degree of local initiative had left one in a pitiful state while the other had flourished.

A team of reporters journeyed to the north of Norway to gather information about an initiative introduced by the Norwegian government. Graduates' student debt was cut by 25,000 kroner for every year they spent in Tromsø or Vardø, the areas of Norway subject to social deprivation. And we visited Gotland in Sweden to see what happens when a government decides to move civil servant positions out of the capital and into the provinces.

The series of "Denmark on the Brink" ("Danmark Knækker") programs and news items culminated in a political debate, but not a normal one. We invited seven politicians and three businessmen to a building that was once a water tower, and has been converted into a museum and which, from its seven-story summit, commands views of some of the most deprived areas in Denmark.

Their participation was conditional on two things: They had to stay for 24 hours, and they had to agree to try to author an action plan that could address the problems that deprived areas in Denmark are subject to. "You're very naive," was the response of one of the experienced politicians when he reluctantly agreed to participate. The then home secretary, the science minister, the then leader of the Socialist People's Party (Socialistisk Folkeparti) and later secretary of state, a member of the Danish People's Party (Dansk Folkeparti), the chairmen of Local Government Denmark and Danish Regions, and the mayor of the host town of Tønder all agreed to spend 24 hours in front of the cameras along with three business leaders. They were part of a national political and media experiment.

Can politicians and businessmen spend that amount of time together and agree, despite their differing interests and party-political affiliations, if the challenge they all face is clear enough and well enough documented? Can the press provide the framework for a solution rather than a conflict? Do Danes have an interest in such a lofty debate? A debate without the intention of showing lots of people arguing bitterly with each other?

Initially all parties showed considerable scepticism. Could they really work together in a completely new way? And could journalists really limit themselves to providing the framework and refrain from trying to influence the result? And could the participants avoid taking the opportunity for point scoring?

A TV journalist hosted the debate, acted as chair, and in the hectic final minutes, functioned as a secretary, taking dictation so that the ten participants could manage to sign the declaration before the 17:00 deadline.

And yes, they agreed that it was a problem that politicians could and should address. Tired but proud, they signed a declaration to that effect at the base of the old water tower. All the participants were surprised by themselves that they had managed to reach agreement, an agreement that was to tie them closer together in the coming years.

This constructive news was quickly sent out to the entire country through radio news shows, 24-hour TV news, DR's website (dr.dk), regional radio stations, regular TV news broadcasts and a number of written media that were following the debate. The results were faster broadband Internet to outlying areas, grants for entrepreneurs, better access to credit for projects in outlying areas, the removal of outdated restrictions and red tape affecting businesses, and better support for students who commute from outlying areas. The panel defended these recommendations a couple of hours later in front of 700,000 viewers and a selected local audience on a live TV show. Never before has DR received so much positive feedback from all over the country, so many comments, suggestions and ideas designed to stop Denmark from losing touch with its outlying areas.

The following year, DR invited a number of healthcare spokespeople to prioritise healthcare initiatives as the culmination of a series of programs dedicated to the sharply rising costs of treating the illnesses that an aging population was refused to die from.

When teachers were locked out of the Danish classrooms during a six-week conflict with the government, we spent three days in a row on our new afternoon show to bring the parties together. We invited a mediator to help the teachers' union and the politicians to understand each other. We brought teachers, headmasters, parents and school kids together to debate what was needed to change in order to improve the education in the country. And we asked new questions of the conflicting parties. Instead of handing them the microphone to argue why the other one was to blame, we wanted to know if they understood the viewpoint of the opposing party, where they could see a compromise, and what their vision for the school system was. It turned out that they did not sign any peace agreement in the studio, but viewers found out what the conflict was really about and learned something, instead of just watching a boxing match.

Far from Borgen

One of the new programs I am most proud of, is "Langt fra Borgen" ("Far from the Parliament"). It was the result of an ambition to fundamentally change the journalistic approach in a weekly current affairs program on politics. In the world of TV, the concept of "hard talk" is the standard hard-hitting political journalist interviewing a so called "victim", meaning a politician. And the idea is a bullfight: Who will win? Will the journalist be able to get the politician to contradict himself, admit he is wrong or at least make him look visibly uncomfortable?

We had become increasingly tired of that concept. Not much came out of it, and most guests were media trained to avoid answering the questions, and the journalists insisted or interrupted, but viewers hated it.

Instead we had the idea of inviting two politicians with different views on a political subject and then bringing them out in Denmark to experience the real world. And instead of critique as the engine in the program, we used curiosity.

First of all, viewers for the first time saw politicians from different parties actually like each other and behave like real people.

Secondly, you saw politicians sometimes change their minds when being confronted with real people with real problems. And thirdly, viewers understood the nuances, that an issue had different sides, and they started doubting their own opinion.

In one episode, two politicians with different views on the future legislation on prostitution, were invited into a brothel to discuss if

Denmark should follow Germany, where prostitution is legal, or our other neighbour Sweden, where prostitution is illegal.

The politicians, and with them the viewers, met a 35-year-old bright woman, who argued that she had a respected job she was proud of, as she felt she could do good for her clients.

"I do this of my own free will. Why can I not pay taxes?"

Then it was difficult to be 100 percent against legal prostitution. But next the politician met a woman who said she had to sell anal intercourse 13 times a week to pay for her drugs. Then it was suddenly difficult to be 100 percent in favour of legalising prostitution.

The result: People were in doubt, and that leads to far more engaged conversation than the traditional one-angle programs or articles on either the crook or the victim; the happy hooker or the traded sex slave and her pimp.

Today, the weekly political magazine on DR1 has more viewers than the old concept of political boxing. In 2017, it won the award at the national TV Festival as Best Current Affairs Program.

The Night of Democracy

And the full-blown boxing metaphor was also what the commercial competitor TV2 introduced to the national election in 2011. The candidates were invited into a real sport arena with thousands of spectators all around dressed in either blue or red t-shirts. There was smoke, loud disco music, half-naked cheerleaders and a bell in the boxing ring, which the popular news anchor would hit if any politician talked for more than 30 seconds.

At DR, some managers feared the competition and suggested that DR had to do something like that in order not to lose the battle of the ratings. But if the media puts a democratic debate into a boxing ring, politics becomes boxing, and that was not our job.

We had another idea: We invited 1,800 voters from all over the country to the DR Concert Hall, and asked for their input to which challenges they wanted their politicians to meet. We had all party leaders on the beautiful stage, where it is just impossible not to behave in a civilised manner. The debate in prime time on the main channel had far more viewers than the boxing event from the competitor.

"Night of Democracy" has ever since become a national tradition leading up to any national election, where DR celebrates with voters, viewers and party chairmen, that we all live in a country where we can elect our own leaders.

Children's Programs

In 2013, DR launched a new TV Channel, DR Ultra, for children between eight and 12 years old. One of the programs showing kids and their parents that this was something new was called The Ultra House. It was a reality show, but in a positive way: Normal school children told each other about a problem they faced. For instance, that they were being harassed, they were unhappily in love, their friends forced them to smoke or drink, or their parents were getting a divorce. The idea of the program was that the children would help each other, with the help of an adult, to talk about and get advice on how to deal with the problem they – and most likely many of the viewers – were up against. In contrast to other reality programs, nobody was sent home. In the Ultra House, they all belonged.

In the autumn of 2013, we launched another program on our main channel DR1 in which four immigrants moved into the homes of native Danes with the task to learn the difficult Danish language. In the process, viewers learned how important a common language is for integration, but also how difficult it can be. As a result, both the immigrants and the ethnic Danes got to know one another, and new friendships flourished.

We launched a series on green energy, and showed in articles on the web, stories on the radio and programs on TV, how people saved money and helped the environment by changing their behaviour.

In 2011 and 2012, we worked together with the think tank, Monday Morning, to find new Danish heroes; and not just those who are good at repeating others' successes and singing other peoples' songs. We called the competition Growth Factor (called VæxtFaktor in Danish which sounds a lot like X Factor) where entrepreneurs compete with each other in front of three judges to prove who has the greatest potential to bring more jobs and income to Denmark. Over three prime time slots, we were told the stories of the resident of the Danish island of Bornholm who now supplies liquorice to companies around the world, the genius from west Jutland who can eliminate a fifth of the world's food wastage with a simple, high-tech temperature sphere for corn silos, the resident of Skagen, who delivers fish door-to-door throughout the country, and the French-Danish man who founded a company that is now in the process of selling electronic patient records software not just to Danish hospitals, but to hospitals all over the world.

No conflicts, no villains and no victims. Just entrepreneurship, commitment, innovation and the will to make a difference. Is that a journalistic cocktail for good TV? Absolutely, at least if you ask the one out of ten Danes who watched the show three weeks in a row – among them a teenage mother who sent this message to the program's producer:

"It's really great that you make programs like VæxtFaktor that can inspire young people. We and our children really enjoyed the shows. Finally, something everyone wanted to watch and which can help to move our society in the right direction – we can't all make a living only singing and dancing ..."

Paradigm Shift

This reaction would come as no surprise to Maja Dalsgaard or Tine Møller Pedersen, who wrote a dissertation at Roskilde University about constructive news when completing their Masters in Communication.

On the basis of thorough focus group tests of a number of TV news broadcasts in 2009, they concluded that: "The recent implementation of several positive and solution-oriented constructive news items has been popular." And furthermore, noted that "Our analysis shows that negative and dramatic news makes many women nervous and men irritated – and without informing them. Many Danes are fed up of negative news items and "emotional pornography." Stories about potential solutions catch people's attention better, because they give the impression that it's possible to do a lot about all the problems that journalists are so good at finding. Constructive news' greatest strength consists in creating better and more qualified debate."

The ambition to inspire is now a key part of DR's overall strategy and its influence has spread beyond the newsroom. Like when DR, a couple of years ago, 'Shrank a town' and followed provincial town Ebeltoft's fight against obesity. We broadcasted new shows where ordinary Danes helped people make tough choices in their lives.

In both TV and radio shows, constructive news has been introduced as a supplement to the traditional news criteria. The goal is for each of the major TV or radio news shows to carry at least one piece that has been angled constructively. Even though DR is aware that it still has a lot to learn, it perseveres and continues to hold courses and experiment with form and content.It is no longer just an editorial decision to put a constructive angle on the day's stories, these changes have trickled down to reporters for whom these stories have started to become routine.

Viewers have also noticed the difference, as DR's media research department can document. For the first time in ten years, a representative sample of the population now associates words such as trustworthy, relevant, informative, constructive, useful, solution-oriented and socially responsible with the 9:30 p.m. TV Avisen, the country's most popular TV news show, and to a much greater degree than a competing channel's output, which, on the other hand scored highly for adjectives such as exciting, fascinating and, not least, entertaining.

At DR News, we believed that leadership is performed by praising what you want to see more of, instead of only criticising the things you do not like. So we started to give out prizes to the best critical and constructive examination paper at the national Journalism School. Internally, DR gave a prize to the best constructive news story; the first one in 2012 went to a reporter who wrote a story about a father wanting to help his son with autism. Imagining his son's future in a society where everybody focused on all the things his son was not able to do due to his handicap, the father took action and gave up his job to start a consultancy firm called The Specialists, which only hires people with autism, and helps them work as consultants in software companies, banks, audit companies and supermarkets – as autistic individuals are often better than the average person at focusing on numbers and details. The Specialists has now expanded to 13 countries, and the story dealt with the father's new vision to hire more than one million people with autism worldwide before 2020 – focusing on the abilities of people instead of their limitations.

Much to their surprise, this was also the lesson learned by the reporters of the regional radio in Copenhagen, DR P4, in 2013. For one week that autumn, they decided to experiment with their journalistic approach and focused on stories with constructive angles in "The Week of Yes". And editor Kathrine Asp Poulsen recalls that the feedback from listeners was amazing: "We have never engaged listeners so much before. Our mailbox exploded with encouragements to continue." One listener, Ann-Britt Braunscheier, wrote:

"What a great idea. As spoken from my heart. The world might not be better if we ignore the problems. But it never improves if we stay down in the black hole of negativity."

Jette Lauritsen wrote: "Remember that you can be both critical and positive." And Claus Rosenquist represented many citizens of Copenhagen when he asked: "Please continue this genius idea of a "Week of Yes". Incredibly good radio."

Easy for You

At conferences outside the Nordic countries, I often get the question from frustrated journalists and editors that they come from countries with many more problems and that constructive news might only work in rich welfare states.

"In the Arab world, there are so many problems that we have had to launch a news channel to find space to cover them all," the editor-in-chief of the international media company Al Arabia Nagle Al Hague said. However, this comment was challenged by a member of the audience who asked:

"But isn't there an even greater need for stories that inspire to solutions when you broadcast in societies full of challenges?"

Here are three examples of how DR tries to implement constructive news angles in foreign coverage:

- During the migrant crisis in 2016, with thousands drowning in the Mediterranean Sea, DR reported live from Malta and aired a report from West Africa, where African and Spanish authorities since 2008 have successfully stopped a wave of boat refuges trying to reach Europe through the Canary Islands and at the same time given aid to the African villages, where the refugees came from.
- We did a story from Israel where a Jewish and a Palestinian family had been neighbours for decades and the story simply told how they coped in an environment where hate, fear, tall walls and war seem to be the norm.
- During the so-called Muhammad cartoons crisis in 2005, when fanatic Muslims around the world protested against the publication of drawings of the prophet Mohammed in the Danish newspaper Jyllands-Posten, most TV stations showed live pictures from Islamic demonstrations in the Arab world. In Denmark, the political reality soon became that the Muslim world hated Denmark, and Danes now were in danger everywhere in the Middle East. Yes, the Danish Embassy in Lebanon was put on fire; yes, there were demonstrations with burning Danish flags and hard rhetoric from Muslim leaders, but were Muslims in the millions really on the rise against little Denmark, as pictures of big fire symbols in capitals in Indonesia, Pakistan, Egypt and Lebanon showed in the newspapers and on TV? Or was the truth that there were protests, but that the news cameras only pointed to the not more than a few hundred, who demonstrated in the big cities, whereas the vast populations in the Muslim communities did not care much about what newspapers thousands of miles away in Denmark published? One answer came when DR sent a reporter to walk the streets of Beirut carrying a giant Danish Flag, and absolutely nobody reacted.

- DR correspondent in the Middle East, Puk Damsgaard, did a prime time TV special on the main channel, DR1, on the conflict in Egypt, where she put three representatives of the different fighting groups on a boat out on the Nile and challenged them to listen to each other and come up with a compromise for a future in Egypt in which they could all see themselves. It was a great story, and also showed how difficult it is to make the conflicting Egyptian parties realise that they are all in the same boat. The program further revealed where the opponents, in the aftermath of the Arab Spring, fundamentally disagree and where future common ground might be found.

It might not be easy, but it is possible to add constructive thinking to the coverage of even the most troublesome areas on Earth.

Are you crazy?

When I first made my thoughts about constructive journalism public in 2008 in a comment piece in the Danish broadsheet, Politiken, they were met with equal measures of curiosity, indulgence and head shaking.

Was the man trying to turn serious news media into happy TV? Was it a conservative attempt to defuse critical journalism? Or was it a sort of naive attempt by a happy-clappy dreamer to "heal the world"? A sort of drivel journalism, like 'above it all the sun always shines'?

"Shouldn't you have become a priest instead?" I was asked on direct TV by the nationally famous news anchor Reimer Bo Christensen.

"Eh ... well, no. Constructive journalism is not a religion, and all I ever wanted was to become a good journalist."

In a Masters dissertation on the subject of constructive news, which the then vice-chairman of the Danish Union of Journalists, Fred Jacobsen, published in 2010, a number of media figures were interviewed about their opinion of the new concept.

"When I hear the words constructive journalism, I get this sense that someone can't face the unpleasantness that's out there in the real world. And my stomach turns. We can't just put a positive spin

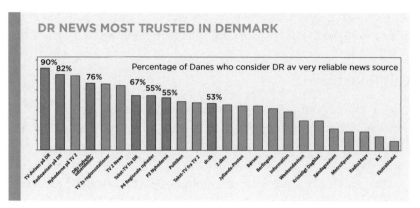

DR NEWS MOST TRUSTED IN DENMARK

Percentage of Danes who consider DR av very reliable news source

90% 82% 76% 67% 55% 55% 53%

Source: Megafon

on things to please people. It's an artificial construct; false," said then Berlingske Media director and editor-in-chief and chairman of the Danish School of Media and Journalism, Lisbeth Knudsen.

Seven years later she is now CEO for Monday Morning, a magazine with the constructive mission of helping companies share best practice and serve "audience navigation" rather than "information".

Danish TV2's news director at that time, Michael Dyrby, was also a declared sceptic, stating in the report that "Our role isn't to be part of some problem-solving team." In 2016 TV2 implemented what they call "19 Inspiration" – a daily constructive story on what is working well around Denmark.

"And every survey shows that our viewers love those stories," Jacob Kwon, the new editor-in-chief says today. But in the early years of the concept of constructive news, other editors struggled to find their own opinion on the whole idea, and in a blog in July 2013, former editor of the Danish tabloid daily, BT, Peter Brüchmann looked back on his years as a news executive:

"I admit it: We are brought up to be negative. It is better to go after the crook than to find the hero. In my world, the work of Woodward and Bernstein is the finest. And at home we applaud those who lift the top off the scandals ... It is the DNA of journalism. And you just don't change your DNA. I tried to introduce just one positive story per day in our newspaper, which we would call 'The success of the day'. We didn't make it every day, and the project died quietly and too soon after a long period of not working. Not quite a success."

Gut Reaction

The most interesting example of a gut reaction came when a Danish version of this book was published in 2012 and the DR late night TV show, Deadline, covered the event the way they normally would in those days:

They invited the most critical public debate provocateur to review the idea of constructive news with me in the studio. In just nine minutes I was accused of being a right-wing politician, a North Korean communist and a journalistic terminator with the purpose of pulling every tooth out of watchdog reporting – all at the same time. In the debate, I felt I had two choices: Either to turn the debate into just another TV bull fight and attack author Carsten Jensen for doing exactly what was wrong with journalism – destroying the debate with aggressiveness – but thereby contradicting my own message of being constructive. Or I could try to defend myself and only leave time to explain what constructive journalism is not. I do not know if this debate had a winner or loser. I was certainly not the winner, but I will say that the viewers probably lost.

It is possible that the result was entertaining, but hardly anyone had any chance of understanding what the idea really was all about. I wonder if many politicians and other people invited to debates on TV do not leave the news studio with the same empty feeling of not having a chance to explain what is really on their mind.

The episode shows that the implementation of constructive news at DR did not happen instantly. The now former DR reporter, Kristian Sloth, remembers the internal reaction on the new ideas from the boss.

"We thought you were crazy," says Sloth, who is one of the most experienced investigative reporters in Denmark and feared among politicians and industry for his hard hitting and often aggressive journalism. He has won several prizes for his reporting, and an interview with a member of the Danish government who went more than a little crazy in front of rolling cameras during an interview with Kristian Sloth is still one of the most shared Danish videos on YouTube.

Sloth dares to say what most of his colleagues, both inside and outside of DR, thought about constructive news when I first introduced it in 2008.

"We made jokes about it, because it is really provoking for a reporter who wants to reveal important matters and has to fight a growing number of spin doctors and PR guys every day, who try to prevent us from doing our job to uncover the truth. Power always tries to paint a positive picture of itself, and our job is get behind those curtains.

"We told each other that it is not our job to do stories about the 200 planes which do not crash, but to report on the one falling from the sky. And I still believe that. But I must say I now better understand what this is all about. Journalism is about telling the truth. It is our job to look for the broken stuff – but the downside is seldom the whole truth. Often there is an upside and a way out, which we should also look for. We have to balance our reporting if we want to live up to our responsibility to the public. If we only look for problems, we leave people in the dark. We need to also build on top of that and look for ways out."

What Do Others Do?

Kristian Sloth for years uncovered the consequences of the transformation in the agricultural sector from traditional farming to a highly effective modern production industry. There are now four times as many pigs in Denmark as people. And pork is one of the most important exports for the national economy. One of the favourite subjects was the growing use of antibiotics in order to prevent the industrial pigs getting ill from living too close to each other in the stables.

The problem was not only the risk of getting penicillin in the bacon and the growing cost of medicine for farmers, the main problem was the resistance to antibiotics among the general human population. In news program after news program, doctors have warned against the heavy use of antibiotics and the risk at hospitals when patients can no longer be cured for their inflammations, because penicillin is no longer effective. But the use of antibiotics and the problem of resistance just increased.

DR and the reporter behind these stories were not popular among farmers: "Why don't you instead do stories on the billions of Danish kroner we benefit to society by our growing export?" they asked. We had to tell them that uncovering problems was our job, and we continued to do more stories on the misuse of antibiotics on Danish farms.

Until one day, when the hard-hitting reporter and his editor decided on a different approach: We wanted to find out if the problem could be solved. Had anyone anywhere experienced the same problem and been successful in coping with it?

In the Netherlands the reporter found a farmer who almost lost his young daughter to a banal infection from a multidrug-resistant bacteria (MRSA). The girl got the bacteria from the pigs – and the bacteria had become resistant to antibiotics due to the father's heavy use of antibiotics on the pigs. Therefore, the antibiotics had no effect on the bacteria and the girl became very ill.

Her father had grown pigs on their family farm and like any modern farmer, put penicillin in animal food in order to prevent them from becoming ill. After his daughter became ill, the farmer, Eric van den Heulen, decided to dedicate his life to find an alternative to antibiotics in pork production. The results of his endeavour seem successful as he now only uses 95 percent less antibiotics than he did just a few years ago. He simply outcompeted the bad bacteria by spraying his stables and the pigs with millions and millions of good bacteria, called probiotics. The probiotics proliferate in the environment and replaces the pathogen (infection-causing) bacteria, and consequently, it prevents the pigs from getting ill and therefore means that they do not need as much antibiotics.

DR ran the story in April 2013 and a few months later major Danish farmers, researchers in microbiology, and a worldwide Danish developer of enzymes and additives to food have decided to copy the Dutch farmer.

"This could turn out to be a stroke of genius," says professor in microbiology at the University of Southern Denmark, Hans Jørgen Kolmos.

"Instead of killing the bad bacteria using antibiotics, you supply good bacteria. It is really thinking outside the box, and I am sure we can use this new method to benefit heath care in general."

"It was probably the most important and constructive piece of journalism I have seen on my TV," says Martin Rishøj, who has worked in the farming industry for decades. After watching the newscast on DR1, he initiated a project in Denmark which copies everything the Dutch farmer is doing, and according to him:

"The results on a few participating pig farms after a few months are very promising." For journalist Kristian Sloth, the experience has taught him something interesting:

"After spending years and years reporting about the downsides in modern farming – and believe me, they are numerous – it felt good to do a constructive story about a man, who actually almost completely got rid of antibiotics through a very simple method. It felt good to do a constructive story with an impact that almost immediately inspired the industry. The constructive story is not a beautiful painting saying all is well. To understand the solution, you first have to understand the problem. So the constructive story contains the problem – but it takes us a step further because it shows a possible solution to the problem. The idea about constructive journalism has had an impact on DR. Some people still laugh about the whole thinking sometimes, but nonetheless, today we see more stories from DR News with an upside or a solution built into the plot." Sloth sums up the new editorial news culture at DR News:

"The hard-hitting and tightly angled revelation with one single crook is not always the way to tell a story. In fact, the effect can be much stronger if the viewer thinks: I've got the pros and the cons – now I can make up my own mind. It is healthy for us and for our customers if we also look for the other story, for the upside story, which will bring us as a society one step closer towards a solution."

Chapter 5

BEST PRACTICE

"Our Republic and its press will rise or fall together ...
A cynical, mercenary, demagogic press will produce in time a people
as base as itself. The power to mould the future of the Republic will be
in the hands of the journalists of future generations."

Joseph Pulitzer, Journalist, in 1883

BBC is the "mother of journalism". What she does must be right. And star struck news people from all over the world go only to visit their giant newsroom to get inspired, to go home and copy what they do.

So, Eva Schulsinger and I were humble in the spring of 2016, when we were invited to talk to the BBC Newsroom. Eva is the very talented and experienced editor of TV Avisen, now the most trusted and biggest Danish evening news program.

We began to show a screen dump of that mornings front page of the BBC News website, which was full of great journalism about how horrifying the world is: (Graphic 5)

Then Eva Schulsinger told the story on how DR News has changed its culture and consequently its news content:

"A few years ago, we had a news meeting planning a series to run in the summer. Someone had the idea of doing a story about Danish teenagers drinking more and more. At the next meeting, he returned with new statistics documenting that in fact Danish teenagers now drink far less than before. The disappointment was huge around the table, but we decided to skip that story and find another problem, with which we could destroy the summertime for our viewers."

Eva told her British colleagues:

Source: BBC.com a random day in the Spring 2016

"Today we would have run that story. And every day we have one, two or more constructive stories in our major news programs. Because they inspire, they enlighten, and they give another feeling to our news flow. In the beginning, I was very skeptical. But now it's a natural part of the journalistic conversation every day in our newsroom."

One year later, BBC News has integrated constructive news in its strategy, calling it "Solutions-Focused Journalism". And BBC World Hacks is one of the results as "an innovative new weekly programme looking at how we can solve the world's problems."

Mega Trend

Since the launch of the first edition of constructive news in November 2011, readers' feedback has been overwhelming. Now with the release of this revised edition and the launch of a German edition, Nathalie Labourdette, EBU leader of Eurovision Academy seems to have a point when she calls Constructive News "the next mega trend in quality journalism":

"Constructive journalism is a new way of thinking. It answers the question of why public media's quality journalism matters to society. It gives our news a clear purpose."

When bright and frustrated reporters and editors have surpassed their natural journalistic skepticism and realised that the vision of constructive news is neither an attack on investigative reporting, nor an ambition of implementing some kind of North Korean positive news approach where important problems are being ignored, then more and more agree that the real crisis in the media industry might not be about eroding business models – but rather about the effect traditional media content is having on news consumers:

People are turning their backs on traditional news reporting, as they no longer find meaning and relevance in the depressing – and falsified – picture of the world, we are presenting to them disguised as news.

But a growing number of news organisations are trying to fight the status quo. They discover a more successful path by adding constructive angles to their news flow.

What's Working

The last few years I have had the fortune to be invited to talk about the need of a constructive change in the media world. For five years in a row, DR has, together with European Broadcasting Union in Geneva invited editors and journalists from public service all over Europe to master classes in constructive journalism.

And after keynotes, seminars, and speeches in at the United Nations in Geneva, Vienna, Hamburg, Brussels, Amsterdam, Oslo, Stockholm, Helsinki, Marrakesh, Prague, Taipei, Tallinn, Riga, Copenhagen and Palo Alto, the message of this book turns out to target a general feeling in many professional journalists – and not only the young, not yet spoiled by our old cynical news culture.

Just listen to Dickens Olewe of the Kenyan newspaper The Star.

When he read the first edition of Constructive News during his Fellowship year at Stanford University in California, he found his life mission:

"There are so many negative stories in the Kenyan press, how about a paradigm shift? What if journalists went the extra mile to highlight the problem and suggest a solution? What if we told more stories of things that actually worked? How would this change our national conversation, how would it impact our democracy and the leaders we elect? The Kenyan media, and by extension the larger African media, must lead the paradigm shift to influence the public conversation for the hope of a better tomorrow. As for me, my passion is finally defined. I'm energised and ready to lead this change," as he explained in his John S. Knight Fellow Blog in early 2015.

Often the sole word "constructive" is perceived not only as an attack on the core journalistic identity but also on the working habits of several generations of news people. But it is possible to change:

A few months after the Swedish-language Yle in Finland introduced constructive stories to their news flow in 2014, and counting more than 400 constructive stories, managing editor Jonas Jungar noticed:

"Overall, we got a positive and enthusiastic response after our decision to implement the concept of constructive news. The audience clearly supports the idea – in a nutshell, the reaction was "Finally!". The initial feelings among our news reporters in the newsroom were more mixed – however, most of them realised the need to challenge themselves and the way they had been doing news for so many years before. Others were a bit more suspicious. They perceived the approach to be a risk, which would make things look better than they actually are. But now constructive news has become an essential part of our editorial toolbox."

The Time is Right

Anne Lagercrantz was editor-in-chief of Swedish Radio News when she made constructive news part of her vision for the future:

"I believe the time is right for a change in journalism. It helps us to rethink the current approach creatively – in a world where so many things in our industry are being turned upside down, and the competition is so intense. Constructive news is definitely not about doing nice and simple stories or to paint positive, but untruthful pictures. It is about providing the full picture."

"Now we are airing stories we otherwise would have not chosen; for example, a story about how the number of people dying from malaria is falling dramatically and why. It has been very rewarding to discuss among ourselves what good journalism actually is. The crisis in the media business and changing consumer habits forces news editors to focus on so much more than on the question what quality really is."

"Haagerup's idea is simple: Journalists do not see the full picture. We have all become tabloid-like in our news routines due to our relentless search for conflicts and drama. Our profession has become used to covering the world in terms of crooks and victims. Constructive news must not be mistaken to be irrelevant or non-informative. It must not lead to the habit of prioritising news that is not important. In the beginning, this worrying assumption has been put forward in the debate on constructive news in Sweden. But by being impartial and trustworthy we are obligated to report on the full picture, and that picture rarely consists solely of misery."

Anne Lagercrantz is now heading the news at public Swedish TV station, SVT, where she took over from News Director Olov Carlsson, who made constructive journalism part of the daily conversation in the Stockholm newsroom:

"The results are good," he explained in 2016.

"One example of this is that SVT has completely rearranged its foreign coverage.

"Instead of only covering famine, war and catastrophes, SVT are now regularly capturing events that depict democratisation, development and hope for the future.

"One of those examples is the coverage on Africa. Now SVT regularly documents signs of life force and positive examples of the 'new' Africa.

"The reception of this development has not always been positive. Both governments and aid organisations have criticised us for disturbing the image of crises and catastrophes. They claimed that it was our intent to decrease the desire among the general public to donate money for contributions to victims in times of hardship.

"But this must never become the purpose of journalism – we are to depict the truest image of reality that is possible. And reality contains both hope as well as despair; war as well as peace; and darkness as well as light. Without one the other cannot exist.

"It is our task to report and depict reality, and this approach has been very well received by the audience.

"People want hope and information, but are also interested in the exposure of crooks and corruption. It is our task not only to depict negative situations, but to point towards possible ways forward and show good examples as well."

Björn Soenens, former editor-in-chief of Belgian public broadcasting "VRT" attended the very first master class on Constructive News at DR in Copenhagen in 2014. At home, Björn held several workshops, and I did a small talk. He implemented a constructive strategy with his staff: One year later, the Belgian news leader looked back on the results:

"Implementing constructive news stories has helped VRT News to achieve higher standards in journalism. It is better journalism, deeper journalism, multi-layered journalism, more engaging journalism. Many of our viewers share these constructive stories on social media. It helps them stay interested in the world. It helps them to move away from the misery model of the world. Constructive journalism has given a boost to many researchers to find better stories as well as new angles to their stories. It helped them to move away from what all the others are doing.

"VRT News got universal praise for a series on Africa, called 'The Other Africa'. The stories showed how Africa is rapidly growing, both culturally and economically. This development takes place far away from the madding crowds that see Africa as a single bundle of war, hunger and poverty. There is so much more out there. We try to show this reality every single day in our newscasts. This way we try to re-define the news.

"Many journalists from other media maintain that journalism should continue to do what it has always been doing: looking for crooks, trouble and conflict, and be critical of all power and autho-rity. Just that. As an editor-in-chief, I was even personally attacked for preaching about constructive journalism in the outside world. Other press outlets misrepresented and framed constructive stories as positive journalism. They claimed that VRT News was closing its eyes to all the things that go wrong in the world. They even called me "sick in the head" and through a big headline, titled "News Boss under attack" tried to have me removed from my position."

VRT still works with solution-focused journalism, but the attacks on Björn Soenens for not being critical enough continued, and he now serves a correspondent in New York for VRT.

A Way Out

In Taiwan, journalism school, public service media and the com-mercial news organisation invited me to a one-day conference on constructive news in one of the big conference centres in Taipei. This country of 23 million people has 13 competing 24-hour news channels and 110 live TV-vans that chase ambulances in the capital to report quicker from the breaking news than their competitors.

"The competition for attention, viewers and advertising money has gone too far for all of us," the chairman of one of the big commercial satellite-TV companies said bluntly.

"It is crippling the democratic debate in our country. But we don't know how to get out of the race with more and more breaking news, more noise and ever shorter news clips. We think the idea of con-structive news might be a way out."

In 2017, the media in Taiwan have trained journalism students and staff on more inspirational journalism and I was proud to be asked to give out the first ever Chinese Constructive Award among entrees from Taiwan, China, Singapore and Malaysia.

A New Role for the Press

As a young reporter working for the Danish broadsheet, Jyllands-Posten, it was my job to find an angle on the continual fights between the government and the opposition.

The 80s was also a time of crisis in Denmark, and the then Prime Minister Poul Schlüter's minority government and the Social Democratic opposition were fighting in public about whose responsibility it was that the necessary decisions hadn't been taken to drag Denmark back to its feet. For months, news coverage had focused on getting political leaders to throw metaphorical rotten tomatoes at each other, while they ensconced themselves ever more securely in their trenches.

I spoke with the then editor of the Sunday edition, the outstanding Jens Kaiser, about a possible angle, and we agreed that it was perhaps a generational issue. Older politicians were getting bogged down in routines and prejudice. The upcoming generation of politicians were born at a time when the welfare state was well developed; they had all gone to state schools and didn't have the same political allegiances and fixed ideas as their predecessors. Perhaps they had something different to contribute.

A bit of research turned up the fact that many of them had jobs that you wouldn't have expected, given the youth wings they led. The chairman of the centre-right Danish Liberal Party's youth wing was an apprentice printing plant worker, the chairman of the youth wing of centre-left party, the Social Democrats, was studying at a business school, whilst the chairman of the Conservative Peoples Party's youth wing, the most right-wing of the established Danish parties, had what is (in Danish) the rather working-class-sounding name of Brian.

All in all, it added up to be interesting story.

I then had the idea of bringing the youth wing leaders together to see whether they were able to reach the compromises that the leaders of the parties they had joined were unable to, and to find a middle path between the Social Democrats' 'Growth in the 90s' and the right-leaning parties' 'Plan for the next century'.

We decamped to a conference venue and spent 24 hours trying to work things out. During the first few hours the young people didn't get much further than attempting to take on the role of real politicians, politicians who knew their party's policies back to front, and attempted to score points from their opponents and to get the journalist to angle the story in their favour.

But when the journalist suddenly changed role, so did the character of the debate. I made it clear to them that we could not use the story unless they managed to reach agreement. Success was not to be measured in terms of confrontation, but in terms of agreement. I was not going to get involved in what they agreed upon, but I would help them to listen to each other and to find a common interest where one existed. My role was no longer that of boxing match referee or secretary, I was their mediator and facilitator.

It proved possible to overcome the vast majority of their disagreements when the young people recognised that the aim of the game was to deliver a better future for Denmark. In the early hours of the morning, the whole project was on the point of collapse over a disagreement about pensions. The Social Democrats' young leader wanted pension contributions to be obligatory and pension provision to be state-organised. Others wanted to give Danes the freedom to choose their own pension fund.

The chairman of the centrist party, the Danish Social-Liberal Party's youth wing Lars Nielsen, who is now a member of DR's board, and the man who would later in life become Denmark's minister of business, Brian Mikkelsen, devised a compromise arrangement in the early hours of the morning. Pension contributions would be obligatory, but Danes would have the option of choosing between a number of approved pension providers. The representatives from the Social Democrats and the Danish Liberal Party approved the plan over breakfast. In less than 24 hours, the party's youth wings had managed to reach the agreement that their parliamentary leaders had failed to for months.

The text of the compromise agreement was sent to party leaders and three of them declared, to our surprise, that it was a compromise they could agree to. One party leader took a long time in sending a response, but eventually refused the deal.

So, no miracle occurred, but Jyllands-Posten had a great constructive story for its front page, and a seed had been sown.

24 Hours for North Jutland

At the Danish regional media house NORDJYSKE, we regularly covered the developing fight between 12 tourist associations who were all trying to tempt Norwegian, Dutch and German tourists to visit their area during the summer months. Tourist numbers were disappointing across the board, and none of the tourist associations had enough marketing resources. The region they covered was also one in which jobs in all the other sectors were being outsourced in record numbers: the shipyard had closed, Flextronic had closed, the meat processing plant had closed.

We decided to try a little experiment. We invited six local mayors, who were also the chairmen of their local tourism associations, to a holiday cottage on the west coast of Denmark. Under the heading 24 Hours for North Jutland we broadcast direct TV news and radio, as well as providing regular net updates on the six mayors attempts to find a solution to the problem NORDJYSKE had set them: How do we double the number of tourists and tourism jobs in North Jutland within ten years? It was an ambitious goal and all parties were aware that it wouldn't be possible to achieve it unless they were prepared to make radical changes.

With the editor-in-chief taking on the role of moderator, and the local population watching and adding their own contributions to the debate on the Internet, the six mayors managed to reach an agreement. They decided to co-found a joint tourist board for the entire region that would market it as one entity and attract greater numbers of tourists. "To the benefit and joy" was NORDJYSKE's mission statement, and the 24 hours for North Jutland project showed we meant it.

We repeated our success, when, after months of political disagreements about the future of state schools, we invited three national politicians, a headmaster, a teacher, a parent and the chairpersons of the powerful representative organisations, School and Society and the Danish Union of Teachers, to a school to participate in an experiment we called: 24 Hours for Class 5.C.

The ambition was to get the eight participants to agree, over the course of a day, what class 5.C (due back from the summer holiday the day after) could profitably learn in the coming year that would qualify them for a job in the global marketplace and a role in a society that would be markedly different to the one that faced the rest of us when we completed our schooling one or two generations ago. What curriculum should they follow?

The then spokeswomen from three political parties participated in a lively debate. Whilst NORDJYSKE's 24-strong film crew filmed every single word and broadcast it directly to the entire region, including the incident when the chairman of the Danish Union of Teachers, during a debate about the quality of teaching, came out in support of the notion that head teachers were going to have to inspect their colleagues' work in the classroom to ensure that the members were actually doing the job they were supposed to.

Before they took a break for the night, I spent some time with the participants over a bottle of red wine and talked through the day's events. The conversation faltered until one of the politicians said: "We're sitting here discussing whether or not we can trust you. Do you journalists really try not to bring us down? Aren't you there to find fault, split us up and get us to look like idiots like you normally do? Can the press really act in a constructive way and not just judge and accuse? We've just decided to make a go of it."

The next day, the proud participants could report that they had arrived at a compromise agreement and a new curriculum for 5C. It put innovation and creativity at the heart of the curriculum and was designed to allow pupils to accept that they would make mistakes, and that that was okay, and to get them to work together with people with skills they themselves did not possess.

Good News

"I have good news," Arianna Huffington wrote on 12 January 2012 on the website she started seven years earlier. As an innovative frontrunner in the age of digital news publishing, The Huffington Post has challenged both the conventions and financial models of the traditional news industry. In 2013, The Huffington Post became the second-largest news provider in the United States, surpassed only by CNN.

In 2012, Arianna Huffington was ready to challenge the very essence of news reporting: HuffPost Good News was the name of the new online section of the American news website. The ambition was to place a "spotlight on what's inspiring, what's positive and what's working. Huffington Post Good News covers the stories that most media choose not to."

On the first day, Arianna Huffington explained the idea:

"Everywhere around the country, people and communities are doing amazing things, overcoming great odds, and facing real challenges with perseverance, creativity and grace. But these stories are rarely told online, in newspapers, and on TV (especially if you live in a primary state being bombarded with negative attack ads). HuffPost Good News will be using a variety of storytelling tools to bridge the wide gap that separates the world as it is from the world as portrayed by the bulk of media ... The excuse often given by the media is that these stories are 'what the public wants'. Well, we don't believe that and HuffPost Good News will be our answer, and challenge, to that cynicism."

The first edition of HuffPost Good News included a portrait of 29-year-old Sarah Churman who heard her own voice for the first time with the help of a hearing implant – and whose video of the experience captivated millions on YouTube. HuffPost Good News also introduced bloggers on positivity, Desmond Tutu being the first as he movingly recalled the struggle to end apartheid:

"We were always upheld and strengthened by the good news of those whose actions reminded us we are each God's partners in a love and justice that includes all."

A year and a half later, Huffington could see a growing market for this kind of news journalism and explained:

"Simply reporting news about what's broken and what's gone wrong doesn't give a full or accurate picture of what's going on. As we expected, we were far from alone in wanting to share stories of what is working in addition to stories about what's going wrong. In its first month, Good News received 5.6 million unique visitors. And on average, it continues to get nearly 5 million unique visitors, nearly 15 million page views, and 1 million social referrals each month."

The then CEO of The Huffington Post, Jimmy Maymann, has learned two important lessons from the experience with constructive news stories:

"Our statistics show that constructive stories are shared far more than traditional news pieces on social media – which is extremely important for us. There is a huge market for it. It has been highly successful for us. We have found that people really relate to constructive stories and are much more engaged in them compared to traditional news reporting. For instance one of our stories on a new way of funding African companies is being shared and debated. People try to find out if this idea can be implemented elsewhere. And on top of that, it gives a broader – and more correct – perspective on life in Africa. On top of that, it also turns out that advertisers like constructive stories more than any other kinds of journalism. All in all we have evidence to say that this kind of journalism it not only better for the audience and society. It is also good for business."

Jimmy Maymann is now head of the privately funded UN Live project aimed at helping to raise awareness about United Nations and the global Sustainable Development Goals. He also sits in the Board of Constructive Institute.

The New Role of the Regional Paper

At the Danish regional newspaper on the island of Fyn, they will not be surprised by the success of The HuffPost. The Danish regional newspaper, Fyens Stiftstidende experienced a stable and slightly growing circulation three years in a row after implementing constructive news in their core strategy.

The then editor-in-chief, Per Westergård, who stopped in April 2016 and now serves on the board of Jysk Fynske Media and chairs Constructive Institute, has no doubt, when he points to inspiration from the thoughts on constructive news and the following strategic new focus on inspirational news as the key element to this success:

"Often there are light years between what a reader thinks is a good story and what a journalist finds to be a good story. And if you listen to readers they will tell you that the "newspaper always shoots down new ideas, before they have a chance," "the newspaper never lets anyone express a vision," and "the newspaper always focuses on the negative sides of things." "They actually see us as a bunch of dyspeptic, old cheroot munching grouches."

His reflections go further:

"As journalists, we have been brought up to sit at the stands keeping an eye on what's going on in the arena. When anyone makes a mistake, we hit hard. It is written in our journalistic DNA, that we focus on the unexpected, on the things that are out of the ordinary. We write when a person is being run down in a crossover, but not about the thousands of times when people pass without being hit by a car. And we love a juicy exposé, where people with power say one thing and do another. At Fyens Stiftstidende we have asked ourselves if it is possible to supplement the traditional, critical observing role with a more activist approach, where the paper enters the arena to play a role and affect events. Our answer to that question is yes."

Westergård is the kind of editor, who believes that his most important job is to experiment with the role his media has to play to the citizens and society he is paid to serve. An editor who realises that if you go on writing articles, taking pictures and producing the news in the same way that you did last year and the year before, then you will most likely get the loss in circulation that you got last year and the year before.

"Only by constantly renewing the content of the paper, we are able to maintain the importance of it for its readers. And the same goes for our other media in print, online, radio and TV: Status quo is not an option. News in itself is not enough anymore. We have to climb the ladder of value. Tell news, but add perspective, background, interaction, analysis and understanding. We have to help citizens to navigate in a more and more complex society," says Westergård.

The first step in the new constructive strategy was to introduce a series of journalistic formats – a systematic use of articles each with a graphic stamp like 'This is how it can be solved', 'How others do' and '3 good pieces of advice'. These so-called 'constructive signals' are blue, round and easy for the eye to catch. Not on every page, but in every paper.

"The idea in the constructive signals is that the journalist is forced not only to describe a problem. As often as possible he or she has to ask the question: How can I contribute with new knowledge? How can I inspire with experiences from the outside? How can I help with a possible solution?"

Fyens Stiftstidende has also introduced constructive news campaigns like 'More action downtown' in order to help the city center of Odense from dying and 'This is how we'll make a living' in order to engage citizens and politicians in a debate on the regional rising unemployment.

Westergård is a rare animal in the media zoo of endangered spices, he is an optimistic editor:

"Do not think for a moment, that constructive journalism is about the absence of critical reporting. It is not. Readers say we are too negative. They never say we are too critical. They want their paper to be critical. They long for a paper that not only hands the microphone to politicians and business people and reprints the picture they want the public to see. Readers expect us to separate PR, spin and representation of interest from fact. They expect us to reveal disproportions of what power says and what it does. But at the same time readers say: Stop being negative and dyspeptic. Show us there are things in our community that succeed. Give new ideas a chance. Inspire us. Please." The example of Fyn tells us that the new approach creates results.

Die Zeit

In the Hamburg, they are not surprised. The two most respected newsweeklies in Germany, Der Spiegel and Die Zeit, are both based in the north German metropolis – both founded by German icons of post-war journalism. But they are now following two different strategies for content and their businesses seems to be headed in opposite directions.

As Der Spiegel had to fire its two top editors in the spring of 2013 amid a long slump in circulation, Die Zeit was celebrating record sales figures and big gains in advertising. Two different approaches underscore these diverting routes. Der Spiegel has a long tradition for hard-hitting investigative and political reporting, and prides itself on its critical tone. In 2012, ads for the news magazine showed a picture of an editorial meeting with the tag line: "The conference that makes politicians tremble."

The problem is that Der Spiegel is no longer alone in the market of this kind of journalism, and readers have turned their backs on both print and online media. Circulation fell from more than a million in 2009 to 883,000 five years later, and even worse, the number of advertising pages have dropped by half over the past decade. Considering the problems in other parts of the news industry this would not come as a surprise, if it were not for a striking growth of neighbouring Die Zeit. Both Der Spiegel and Die Zeit try to reach similar audiences of affluent, well-educated readers, but their curves point in different directions.

Since 2002 circulation of Die Zeit has gone up by 20 percent, reaching more than 500,000. Zeit Online has in ten years gone up from 3 million hits per month to 31.5 million visitors make zeit.de the fastest growing German speaking online site. Advertising revenue has increased close to 75 percent in 2017, and circulation revenue skyrocketed 58 percent in a decade when newspapers in the rest of the country are dying. Two other German news magazines, Focus and Stern, are also losing circulation. What is going on?

Reiner Esser, media manager at Zeit Verlag has an explanation:

"People in Germany, and maybe in the rest of Europe as well, have become sick and tired of the traditional journalistic approach, where only bad news is good news. Unfortunately, many editors and journalists haven't realised this change. And the consequences for the industry are not good."

Giovani di Lorenzo is the editor-in-chief of Die Zeit, and he thinks other media can learn from the lessons learned in Hamburg:

"20 years ago, Die Zeit was in a real crisis. Circulation was dropping, the reputation of the paper was very problematic. And we had a deficit of 30 million German marks (15 million euros). We had red numbers. And back then we could not blame the Internet. We had only ourselves to blame. So we were forced to consider what we did wrong."

In order to change their situation, Die Zeit changed its journalistic approach, as di Lorenzo puts it:

"A reader experience that consists week after week of finding out how bad the world is, so at the end you only want to pull the blanket over your head, that seems to me to be a rather masochistic exercise."

He continues: "After reading the paper people must feel that they have learned something, that they have won something. Knowledge. But perhaps also an insight that wasn't open to them before, but which make them happy now. In the end, people must feel it paid off. The basic feeling must be: It was good I read the paper. Today, we try to make a mix of stories in Die Zeit, so there are always stories which arouse one's curiosity. Which are a promise of something new, and which perhaps also have a constructive approach. Here readers get a learning approach to a problem, which perhaps can be transformed into other areas."

Spreading the Word

The Danish left-wing daily newspaper, Information, is known for its very critical reporting. Some would call the tone sharp and close to depressing. The edition on Wednesday 17th September 2014 seemed to look like any other, and all the articles dealt with traditional themes in the newspaper: Wars, crises, and environmental problems.

But many readers felt differently that day after reading the paper; joyful and optimistic, and that was the mission. Every article focused on the possible solutions on the problems the newspaper normally only pinpointed and complained about.

One the front page the headline read "One place in Syria democracy lives".

"The cover story showed that it is possible to do constructive and hopeful journalism in even the most hopeless reality. It can be done, and at the same time still practice the critical analysis and normal journalistic criteria of importance," the then editor-in-chief Christian Jensen explained.

He calls the reactions from readers overwhelming. In modern times information hasn't had so massive a response from its readers, and with almost no exceptions they were positive. The traffic on its website was 15 percent higher that day, and the paper received more likes on Facebook than ever before. 300 new users signed up on information.dk.

"The initiative for the special constructive edition came from a – normally very critical – reporter, who started a daily news meeting by claiming that he would never be able to persuade his children to read his own paper, if it was only about problems and death. So we developed a concept and the normal beat reporting groups found the constructive stories. It was not difficult at all. We have learned that if our job is to a give a true picture of the world and the time we live in, we fail if we only focus on problems and decay. Because that is not how the world is," Christian Jensen says.

"We have learned that there is a lot of good journalism in reporting on positive trends created by visionary people, and our job is to find the right balance between problem and solution. We will now continue that journey."

Three days after that new understanding by the most critical newspaper in the Kingdom of Denmark, 40 newspapers worldwide, came to the same conclusion. In what they called "Impact Journalism Day",

Le Soir, The Sunday Times, La Stampa, The China Post and 36 other newspapers around the world published articles about initiatives which create positive changes.

"The role of the press is to keep people informed. But the time is over, when the most important role of the media was to "twist the pen around the wound," as the great French journalist Albert Londres once wrote. In rising numbers journalists want to contribute toward the common good by reporting on solutions and creating hope," the man behind the Impact Journalism Day, the Frenchman, Christian de Boisredon, explains.

"Day in and day out news is full of the problems of the world. The constant stream of bad news makes us worried, afraid or – even worse – numb. But the truth is that citizens, companies, universities and organisations today are more engaged than ever before in solving the problems of the planet. We are witnessing a wave of social innovation and social business projects."

Impact Journalism Day changed the content of news for one day. Now comes the time to supplement the news content on the other 364 days.

New questions

At the Icelandic Public Service Station RUV, the experienced news anchor Helga Arnardóttir was asked to do one more season of a talk show where she and a colleague was confronting a politician or a civil servant. But she was reluctant. She felt that the concept of TV arm wrestling drained her energy and worse, that viewers no longer got any wiser from her very critical approach. So in late summer 2017 she did something new: She asked different questions.

"Instead of fronting the problem first, like we have been taught in the news reporting for decades, we fronted how the problem can be solved. This approach made me understand much more clearly what constructive journalism is all about," Helge Arnardóttir said a few days after the showed aired. She says that normally she would introduce the story like this:

"Roughly 100 people are now waiting for group therapy treatment to treat depression and anxiety in Reykjavik. The services can't respond to this demand because of lack of psychiatrists who offer the sessions.

"This would be a typical news intro to draw up the bleak situation. This is the way we have done it for decades. Just 20 minutes before the interview I wrote my intro in a different way:

"What needs to be done to improve the service in Reykjavik in order to respond to the many people who need to undergo a group therapy session to treat depression and anxiety?

"That rephrasing changed the whole interview. We always offer the problem to our viewers, but rarely cover the possible solutions to the problem. That doesn't mean that journalists should be declared problem solvers to every problem that is reported. We just need to approach the solution to the problem as well in our reporting. The response I got after this 8-minute interview was much different than any other interview we have done before. We are not talking breaking news here, but talking about what to do about a problem was just so much more engaging for people to watch, than our old approach," the Icelandic News Anchor said.

"In a changing TV environment and falling linear TV viewership numbers, we need to use different approaches in order to get the viewers' attention. Research shows that people get tired of hearing of constant negative news and problems. But we as journalists and the so-called 'fourth estate', have obligations to report the problems, ask the questions and demand solutions," Helga Anardóttir says.

"By changing our approach in a constructive way, without taking anything away from our reporting, we might keep our viewers longer and maybe offer a new dialogue between the viewer and the broadcaster."

Takeaway

Everything Begins with a Thought

"Be careful of your thoughts, for your thoughts become your words. Be careful of your words, for your words become your actions. Be careful of your actions, for your actions become your habits. Be careful of your habits, for your habits become your character. Be careful of your character, for your character becomes your destiny."

– Chinese proverb

Chapter 6

HOW TO DO IT?

To see the right and not to do it is cowardice

Confucius, Chinese editor, politician, and philosopher

Remember school? For many of us, the picture in our memory is full of yelling teachers, pointing fingers, and embarrassing red lines under misspellings and wrong calculations. When my son, Anders, came home after the first day of preschool, I was somewhat surprised when he triumphantly threw his new LEGO school bag on the floor and proclaimed:

"That was it!"

"What was what?" I asked.

"I can read and write," the six-year-old responded.

"No, you can't, and you have to go back to school tomorrow, just so you know."

"I know that, and it'll be fun. Because there is a language grown-ups don't understand."

"You mean texting? I can do that – almost," I replied.

"No, it is called children spelling," he proclaimed.

"That's nonsense," I said, handing him a piece of paper and a pen, "Show me!"

He started to write something very fast. The messy lines made no sense whatsoever.

"Read it aloud," I demanded.

Anders proceeded to read his story about two trolls who played soccer and one of them scored a goal in the wrong end. I wondered what this was all about and had a chance to ask the teachers at a meeting with parents later that week. It turned out that they planned to experiment with our children for the next seven years:

"Instead of pointing out the mistakes the children make, we will try to praise the things they do well," the teachers explained. "We will underline the right letters with a blue pen, instead of underlining the wrong ones with red, as we have done for generations." Several of us parents simultaneously rolled our eyes.

"Does that mean that when you ask Anders if he can spell the word Horse, and he answers 'H-P-M-Z-X-T', you will pat his shoulder and say how good it is that he can listen to the sound and figure out that horse begins with an H?"

"Exactly," the teachers answered happily.

"Alright, stop that hippie stuff and start giving them homework so they'll learn to read the right way, the hard way, just like the rest of us did," a father said in a loud voice.

But the teachers believed in their idea and taught the class in the new way. And a strange thing happened; all the children loved going to school, because they were praised for each bit of progress they made. The teachers loved to teach that class because the children were so motivated, and before Christmas every child in the class was able to read – faster and better than any other class in the school area. For the next five years, national tests showed that the class performed better in reading, writing and mathematics than any other class in the district.

Maybe this strategy of praising the good you want more of, instead of criticising the bad stuff, works only on children? Or is the example a hint, not only to schools, but also to other areas where negativity rules?

Trouble Shooting

American professor and motivation researcher, Frank J. Barrett, makes a living from changing the business culture of major American organisations, among them the U.S. Navy. He has helped the Navy leave the traditional military culture – where the boss is always right and the job of an employee is to avoid mistakes. The goal is a new innovative leadership culture where managers lead on the principles of shared values and people are supposed to think for themselves and work together in order to come up with better and faster solutions.

Barrett has written a book, Appreciative Inquiry, which deals with the subject of the consequences of negativity in organisations:

"We've gotten used to, as a society, approaching things in terms of problems. If there's a problem then we – politicians, business leaders, whatever, should address that first. It seems like a logical approach. If someone or something in our organisation isn't working, then our instinct is to analyse the problem and correct it. We do it when we bring up our children, when we teach our pupils and when we manage our staff. Lawyers make their money from finding problems instead of finding solutions. Widely-used management tools, such as TQM [Total Quality Management], focus on avoiding errors, and that gives rise to organisations where staff are reduced to potential risk factors and managers are reduced to experts in troubleshooting. And you journalists do exactly the same," Frank Barret told me.

He finds media organisations interesting because they almost always have an ingrained culture of looking for problems and criticising:

"All you do is look for problems. That sort of culture destroys people and affects a whole society's motivation and makes the innovative solutions we need, difficult to find."

How to Break a Horse?

The word 'management' originates from the French word mesnagement (or ménagement), which in turn derived from ménager, meaning "to keep house", which also refers to taking care of the domestic animals. Also, the Italian word maneggiare, means "to handle", especially of a horse. And so management used to mean how to train horses – if you use the whip like this, the horse will do that. The whole concept of management was exported from the military into the Industrial Age in the late 19th century, as was the organisational structures of the new factories: Just like in the army where the officers did the thinking, gave the orders, controlled the situation so that they obeyed, and punished the soldiers who didn't do as they were told; so too the managers treat their workers. Too many organisations are stuck in this quagmire of the Industrial Age, based on a century-old, inherited, and often well-funded mutual distrust between unions and employers. "The more we can steal from the opponent, the more successful we are, and the more we can keep to ourselves," explains Barrett.

Shortly after I had begun my new position as a boss in the news business, an editor-in-chief of a local newspaper, whispered to me to "Outsmart the journalists before they outsmart you."

That attitude may not create instant trust, respect and results. But in the many news organisations that I have visited all over the world, top management are still seen as cynical bureaucrats who care more about the bottom line than the bylines. And they, in contrast, often see reporters as overpaid, spoiled workers who think that they are artists and therefore, in order to keep their privileges, hide behind unions who behave and sound like the now dead typographers.

I have seen newsrooms where both might be right. But it would be more constructive if managers and employees stopped seeing each other as opponents and understood that they are in the same boat, and that it is downright stupid to stand on each end of the sinking ship and think 'we are glad that the water is not coming in on our end of the boat'. Just imagine if both parties recognised that in order to survive, companies no longer have to compete with puttering cargo barges in regular service, but with modern speedboats which have to ride the rough waves and fight the throw winds of the rocky globalised seas. Just imagine if both parties realised the need for both captains who dare to set a course and adjust it in time, and for skilled sailors who can think for themselves and tighten the sails when needed. And while we are making use of this maritime metaphor, most organisations need seamen who accept that the view is better from the bridge, and for officers who love both sailors and sailing. As the brilliant global business consultant, C. K. Prahalad, once told me:

"There are far too many managers in the world, and too few leaders. And leadership is something completely different. Leadership is creating the future by providing innovation and hope."

And in a work environment where everybody is afraid of being punished or ridiculed by either their boss, their peers or both, people stop taking risks. If you are afraid of failure, you begin to play it safe, and the ideas you express are the ones you can be sure are going be accepted, and in organisations where negativity rules, you begin to copy old successes. However, if you are in a business where new ideas and innovation are essential for survival, this culture is fatal. If you are afraid of failure you will end up becoming a failure.

How to Lead Innovation

New ideas can only grow in a culture where it is okay to make mistakes. As Thomas Edison once said: "I did not make mistakes. I found 9,999 ways in which an electrical light bulb does not work."

One of my good friends is the Danish songwriter and singer Lars Lilholt, who is one of the bestselling artists in the country. He has a clear view on his own skills and creative process:

"I sing so badly that I cannot make a living of singing other peoples' songs. That's why I have to write my own. But the creative process needs healthy and constructive feedback, but mainly just praise. The beginning of my life as a musician happened among Marxists. Nobody got any praise there. Critique was the way to communicate. Nobody dared to do anything that could be criticised. And then you play it safe, and not much new comes out of that."

Historians have found few examples of great innovations in old Europe in the Middle Ages, from the year 900 until 1300. Brutal dictators and a strong church claimed to have all the answers, and questions to the authorities and status quo could be lethal. Only when the plague killed many of the priests, kings, warlords and all other figures of authority, did people dare to ask questions, dream and experiment again. The result was the Renaissance in Europe and an explosion of new ideas, inventions and thoughts.

Culture Change

In traditional business areas such as construction, a shift in culture is on its way in Scandinavia. The dirty little secret in the construction business was that success demanded the ability to calculate, build, and then outsmart the client you were building for. It was a game of poker and tough negotiation. Now some companies are trying to change from the formalistic acting of the Industrial Age, to the concept of 'partnering' – where previously they were opponents, now builders, architects and contractors partner to find the best ideas and solutions at the most cost-effective price.

When I followed negotiation classes at Stanford Business School in the beginning of the 1990s, mediation was still somewhat of a hippie word in the MBA world. But the professor insisted that billions of dollars were wasted in unnecessary conflicts fuelled by greedy law firms who specialised in turning disagreements into costly and time-consuming wars. Instead, he tried to teach the future CEOs a different approach, where the people representing different views were placed on the same side of the negotiation table.

"If you physically sit opposite each other, it will eventually turn into arm wrestling where there is only one winner and one loser. But by putting the problem on the other side of the table you begin working together on how to solve it," the professor said, and taught the students to look for the parts of the solution that mean a lot to the other person, and less to you.

That meant that listening was just as important as talking. It meant that building trust became a key qualification and that fighting negative and aggressive vocabulary became essential.

An example of the impact of this type of mediation is the decline in divorce rates in many Norwegian cities after the introduction of professional mediators who help desperate husbands and wives to save their marriages. Normally troubled couples follow the traditional path and each hire their own lawyer. But experience is that this path leads to divorce, more fights, less trust and too often a very complicated life afterwards with huge problems not least for the children who have to grow up in broken families. By helping the fighting married couples to understand each other in an early state, the government saves a lot of marriages, a lot of pain and a lot of money.

Law schools are not the only faculties to focus on conflicts. Science builds on the principle of critique, as professor Hans Henrik Knoop points out:

"Asking questions and critiquing the status quo is essential to most science. But it is getting out of hand when scientists, by tradition and to be taken seriously by their peers, ignore best practice and the good examples."

The Danish professor in psychology also notices that "Over the last 30 years, 45,000 articles have been published in psychology journals about depression, and just 4,000 about happiness. This mindset influences public debate and political decisions in, for instance, health care, where attention and money goes to treating diseases, leaving very little resources to efforts trying to prevent them."

Gentle in what you do

In journalism, the best reporter is, in the eyes of other reporters, the most critical. We reason that the sharper the questions, the better the story. No wonder many politicians react with 'no comment' or hide behind spin doctors and rehearsed quotes.

We might all learn from exceptions like the American reporter from The Seattle Times I met a couple of years ago. He did amazing interviews, and I learned his secret: When faced by a person whom he wanted to open up and tell him something, the reporter kept his notebook in his pocket for the first twenty minutes of the interview. Suddenly he would take his notebook out of his pocket and say, "could you please repeat what you said just now. It was very interesting and well put."

Then he would write the quote down very carefully in his notebook. And then he did his trick: He would put the notebook back inside his pocket.

"During the rest of the interview, they'd do anything to get me to take that notebook back out of my pocket. So, they think and think to try and find something that's worthwhile and well-articulated. And the interview gets much better," explained the reporter, who instinctively knew that a positive response gives better results than a normal purely aggressive journalistic attitude.

Don't Yell

When I finally had to give in to years of pressure from my wife and children and add a dog to our household, it did not take many weeks before I had to attend a local puppy training class. There, in line with dozens of other new dog owners with barking, crazy and uncontrolled four-legged creatures at the end of too-long leashes, I learned a leadership lesson. All of us frustrated dog owners had come to the class to change our misbehaving dogs – how to make them not sit on the sofa, not eat our socks, not use our shoes as toilets, not to bark into the night, and to come back when asked to. But it turned out that the dog trainer didn't pay much attention to the dogs, she wanted to change us dog owners:

"Don't yell at the dog when it runs away. Never hit it when it misbehaves. Reward the desired behaviour instead. Don't use force. Praise your dog, and help it do the right thing."

The American horse whisperer, Buck Brannaman, became famous when Robert Redford played him in the movie The Horse Whisperer. He opposed the traditional way of 'breaking' wild horses where John Wayne types forced their will on the horse with power, whips and the use of spurs. Brannaman has helped thousands of frustrated owners of horses with troubled minds using a different and more effective approach:

"Try to understand the horse and help it to do the right things," Brannaman urges, and teaches a constructive approach to leadership where the art is to gain the trust of the other party to help find the right solution. "Be gentle in what you do. Firm in how you do it."

Takeaway

Constructive News is Not

- Uncritical
- Superficial
- Naïve
- Irrelevant
- Unsensational
- Blind to the world's problems
- The sweet story
- Politics and activism

Constructive News Offers

- A way out
- Hope
- Inspiration
- Call to action
- Education
- Perspective

Chapter 7

CONSTRUCTIVE LEADERSHIP

*People, who are crazy enough
to think they can change the world,
are the ones who do.*

Apple Commercial "Think different", 1996

Everybody wants progress, but nobody wants change. This truth is well-known by any leader in the world. The best of them understand that if more change happens outside of the company than inside it, the company ends up in trouble.

The massive and rapid changes in media technologies and consumer habits have made change the core of editorial management. Running a newsroom has, in recent decades, meant an endless series of cutbacks, new workflow, implementation of new skills, new organisational models, and hopefully a new culture where the traditional solo I-take-no-shit-where-is-my-morning-whiskey reporter in his curled cotton coat has been replaced by reporter teams, who are not only faster and more skilful, but also have the social capacity of working together with people who are not like themselves.

Change has become a permanent condition: From analogue to digital. From print to web. From broadcast to on demand. From mono media to multimedia. From industry to innovation. From monopoly media to social media. From mass communication to a situation where anybody can tell their own stories in text, sound and video, and reach hundreds of millions of people by doing so.

It is foolish to insist on keeping a collective identity as a gatekeeper, when the fence is gone. Media is Latin for 'through', but people no longer need to go through us anymore for information. They can communicate directly with each other without the need and interference of media. So yes, the sole foundation of traditional media is getting eroded and more than ever media companies, newsrooms and individual editors and journalists need to focus on how to create meaning for people and society at large, in order for citizens to be motivated to spend time and money on journalism. The focus from the traditional critical and negative to the more constructive editorial approach is one strategy with the purpose of creating a new meaning of journalism. Nevertheless, it demands change in identity, in culture, in approach, in workflow, in the questions we ask, in the headlines we write, and in the content we produce.

Is it easy? Don't count on it.

Can it be done? Of course it can.

However, it demands leadership and understanding that any change in routines and news cultures does not come by itself, and cannot be implemented by memos or by direct order. It is not easy to break the habit of a lifetime: 86 percent of us always fall asleep in the same position. 78 percent of us always sit in the same place when we watch TV. 81 percent of us always eat lunch in the same place, at the same time and with the same people.

The Power of Habits

My wife is a doctor, and as a result, our house is always full of innumerable scientific journals, most of which are completely beyond my comprehension. However, one of them caught my eye, and it was an analysis of the power of habit: 1,600 heart patients were told by their doctor that they would die within six months if they did not radically alter their habits, such as eating french fries, smoking, drinking too much alcohol, not doing enough exercise.

What is interesting is that the proportion of patients who can change their habits under threat of death, was only 10 percent. The neurologist behind this scientific article was thus able to conclude that 90 percent of people are unable to alter their habits even though they understand at the intellectual level that not doing so will kill them. Does that help answer the question of why so few companies have survived the financial crisis, and why it is so easy to talk about change, but so difficult to do it?

How many times have you attended a seminar about change readiness and new strategies, only to go on doing things in the same way the next day? Since it feels comfortable, you tend to never find the time to get started on doing things in a new way. Perhaps this is because you know what you have got, and you never know what you might get. Better the devil you know, than the devil you don't. Besides, we are all so busy anyway, who has the time to change?

Here is a brief exercise I want you to try: Clasp your hands. Perhaps while your hands are in this position, you can pray that the changes will pass and never affect you.

Now, look at your fingers, is your left thumb on top of your right thumb, or visa versa? In fact, about half of us hold our hands in such a way that our left thumb is on top. The other 50 percent of us solve this motor control problem by putting our right thumb on top. And it has absolutely nothing to do with whether we are right or left handed, it is just a question of habit; habits that were formed when you were so small that you do not even have any recollection of their formation.

You were lying in your cot fiddling with your fingers and your brain said to itself, 'that worked, now I can concentrate on something else'. Try to put your hands together in the way that the other half of the population does it. You never do it that way, and it feels strange, uncomfortable, unnatural, wrong even, right?

Habits and routines help the brain to tackle other, more important tasks. Think if you had to concentrate on the complicated process involved, for example, in taking a step forward, or buttoning a shirt, or riding a bicycle. Your body knows how to do it, because your routine habits take over. Doing what we customarily do is good, it is only bad if we want to do something new – which will require recognition, willpower and courage from us.

Coping with Conservatives

In many newsrooms in the Western world, unions too often see their role as routine opponents to change as life has taught them that the word change is new management speak for cutbacks, more work and more trouble. Editorial cultures have also had centuries of fighting any authority with critical questions ingrained in their DNA.

This makes an industry that, by its very nature should be fascinated with everything new, to be in fact very conservative and locked on maintaining the status quo. Furthermore, management in the news industry has been dominated by the routine that the best reporter was appointed to become the leader of the other reporters.

Yet, just as the best sales person does not necessary become the best boss of the sales force, or the best doctor becomes the best leader of the hospital, being a good writer, news anchor or copyeditor does not in itself qualify someone to run the speedy changes in a media world in the midst of a paradigm shift.

In fact, most of us editors have gotten our leadership positions because we were good at something else; for instance, I was promoted to my first position as managing editor because I was fairly good at writing long articles. The point is that specialists do not necessarily become good leaders.

The psychologist, Daniel Goleman, writes in his book 'Primal Leadership': "The biggest mistake a company can make is to put the best programmer in charge of the software company – without knowing if he is able to inspire others and communicate efficiently. It will most likely turn into a gigantic failure."

The technical qualifications needed in a specific job do not in themselves qualify someone to the role of leadership where the raw material is people. Leadership is about one thing only: Creating results through other people. Or put in another way, leadership is about translating talent into performance – to motivate people, move them mentally, and help them improve and work together in order to create the framework so that they can use their full potential. It demands the desire to work with other people and is, as such, fundamentally different from the baseline of the specialist as a technical competency.

The desire alone is not sufficient for good management. Although management is a skill that can be taught, there is no guarantee that even several years at a business school and a prestigious MBA title will make someone a good boss. However, an updated management toolbox is just as important as the realisation that one of the most important qualifications of a good leader is being constructive.

The Constructive Leader

- Be authentic – don't play a leader, be one
- Know your own strengths and weaknesses
- Have a positive attitude – give mental high fives
- Have respect for others
- Praise in public what you want more of. Criticise one on one and in private.
- Show a desire for change and challenges
- Be creative, open and hard working
- Be good at collaborating with others who are not like yourself
- Have a sense for quality
- Be able to communicate, inspire and create visions
- Listen louder – bring your ears to work. Not only your mouth
- Don't take yourself too seriously

The most important skill for a leader is to understand what happens with people and organisations when you try to change them.

I believe that a good leader needs to work with four "boxes", security, target, feedback, and pressure, and it is the leader's job to fill each of them in order for every individual to perform optimally in the Innovation Society, where creativity and the execution of good ideas are essential:

Security is the most important. You need to feel welcome and valued. The culture needs to be that everybody speaks properly and shows each other respect. It is okay to make mistakes because you learn from them. The working conditions are good, the salary comes in due time and is fair, and the food is okay. You belong here with us and all of us need what you do.

The **target** is clear. This is the direction in which we work together. This is your task. This is your responsibility. This is what you have the competence to do. These are the expectations. Do we agree on that? When I was at DR, I would emphasize that we needed to tell important stories to the audience, and that going to work has to be great, because if it isn't fun going to work, we cannot produce good stories, and if we do not tell important stories then nobody will want to listen.

Feedback, constantly and both ways: Do we tell good stories and is it fun working here? It has to be part of the daily conversation and not only come up in the annual review. How are you? Are both sides satisfied with the agreement we have? If not, we need to do something, like refreshing the targets, offering courses, and changing workflow. And the model learned at manager courses is to praise first, then critique and praise again – it is not good if it is not honest: "It was good you came here, it was some shit you made, it was good you went back home."

Pressure: There are consequences if you do not meet the targets we agreed upon. If you constantly fail to deliver, then it is not fun for your colleagues who have to do your job as well. And yes, when everything else has been tried, it might be that you do not belong here. Remember there is a reason why you are paid. If, over time, you want more compensation than you create in value, then we end up having a problem, and no union can help you with that.

The non-leader thinks that if only the box with security is full, then results will follow. The psychopath leader, on the other hand, believes that if only people are scared and the box with pressure is as full as possible, then people will work at their best.

However, if the constructive leader remembers to fill up all four boxes of motivation and is always honest in the dialogue about the target, and the integrity of each individual, then everybody works better and we end up getting an improved, and more secure work life.

Strategy: From A to B

In implementing change, the most important task of any leader is to understand, and later communicate, the two pictures:

'The first one I call 'the toilet is on fire'. The equivalent expression in English is "light a fire under them": If they do not feel the heat under them, why would they move? If you do not sense the burning platform, it is much more comfortable and easy to just stay where you are. Better the devil you know ...

But if you *only* make people see the flames under them – and it is not difficult to paint a doomsday picture of the news industry, with declining circulation and dropping sales curves – then you only succeed in depressing people. And apathy and depression do not engage. It makes you stuck where you are, which is a bad place to be if the fire is starting to catch you.

That is why the leader needs to understand and communicate the second picture: The vision – a realistic dream of how tomorrow can be better than today. The road from the first picture to the second picture is what business professors and the expensive consultants call strategy. Successful implementation of a strategy demands that you have a clear picture of where you are, where you want to go, and the involvement of your staff in building the road to get there.

Many editors can tell horrible stories in low voices about how difficult their first years in management were. They soon realised that you cannot lead journalists – while the newsroom budget is getting smaller and smaller – through the needed changes by merely arguing 'because I say so!' or by giving in and letting reporters do what they have always done, but faster.

So, if the editor does not understand that the news routines of modern reporting end up scaring customers away and painting a generally false and too-negative picture of the world (and they are communicating that picture), then the reporters will automatically fight the idea of constructive news as an attack on their identity and the basic notion of critical reporting. Even if you do try to paint that picture, the change does not come easily.

New ideas often experience the same pattern. First, they get ignored, and then they are ridiculed. If they are not dead by then, then they are met with fierce resistance. And if the idea, by chance or sheer stubbornness, makes it and becomes part of the new routine, then most people will say that this is not really new, but that it is something that we have always done.

Or as the German philosopher Arthur Schopenhauer put it:

"All truth passes through three stages. First, it is ridiculed. Second, it is violently opposed. Third, it is accepted as being self-evident."

Where is the Problem?

Nanna Jespersgaard was teaching at The Danish School for Media and Journalism. Being a journalist herself, she was frustrated with the negativity of her profession and wanted to supplement her education of future reporters with constructive story-telling techniques. But her fellow teachers thought that was a very bad idea.

"The critique was either that constructive journalism was not real journalism or that it was not new at all and that everybody already did it. The conservatism and skepticism at that time was immense."

She recalls how she insisted and was allowed only to teach constructive journalism as a test.

"The students got really motivated and good at also finding inspirational stories as a supplement to the problems they uncovered. But then they had internships in the news media, and got absorbed by the traditional news culture. And there was just no demand for constructive stories: Only crime, conflicts and problems."

Nanna Jespersgaard did a masters degree in constructive journalism in her spare time and concluded her study about the conservatism in her profession by quoting from scientific research on animals: "Scared rats do not explore the labyrinth." Now she has quit her teaching job to work with communicating research results from scientists at the department of Health at Aarhus University.

"From here, I can follow how easy it is to get journalists to do stories about new problems. But research which contradicts the myths about how scary the world is, is far more difficult to get attention in the traditional news media."

Challenging a journalistic culture takes time and demands a change in journalism training, admits the Rector of The Danish School for Media and Journalism, Jens Otto Kjær Hansen.

"The critical, negative tradition is so solidly founded that the use of the word 'constructive' alone in combination with journalism easily leads to remarks about silly, positive reporting. Most teachers at journalism schools are just as formed by the negative, critical tradition as everyone else. And new students in journalism have, even before they come here, based their views on real journalism from the media content they already know." Rector Kjær Hansen continues by saying that the education for future Danish journalists is changing and that it is about mindset:

"Most teachers in journalism are just as used to the critical, negative approach as anybody else in the business ... But many people outside are, in their daily life and at work, very positive and solutions-oriented to a degree which we as professionals often ignore due to our negative tradition. There are so many more hits on the web where people help each other, than finding hate sites. No doubt the potential for crowd sourcing is enormous in constructive, critical journalism."

Grumpy for the Sake of It

For many years, DR's news culture could perhaps be best described as 'grumpy for the sake of it'. And in many of the media organisations I have visited around the world, the word 'feedback' has been a daily mantra that editors and their assistants have persistently stated that you could not get enough of. A lot of editorial meetings begin by denigrating others' work and the stories that their competitors have run. The errors made the day before, criticism of the rubbish that ended up being published because the other departments were not doing their jobs properly and their planning was abysmal. And when everyone ends up feeling really worthless, you can bet the person leading the meeting will ask:

"Well, are there any good ideas for tomorrow?" Funnily enough, there often are not.

I have spent years of my life as an editor trying to legitimise my own position by satisfying journalists' demands for more feedback. Subsequently, I have found that this is a sort of code, a sort of way of saying to your manager that "I'd like you to praise my work, please. And I'd like you to do something about the idiots whose work I have to do for them because they always take the easy way out." But in most cultures, it is not socially accepted to say something like that, so instead reporters ask for more "general feedback". It is a much more effective way of managing things by getting involved with stories before they are printed; praise the things you want more of, and behind closed doors, re-engage the enthusiasm of under-performers.

Negativity Impact

Professor of psychology at the University of North Carolina and author of the book Positivity, Barbara Fredrickson, has researched how negativity impacts culture in newsrooms:

"Positive mental conditions create high performance, less illness, more cooperation, greater outlook and better idea generation. None of the journalistic newsrooms I have belonged to in 12 years have seen it as an asset to be positive. On the contrary, being positive has been a word associated with the naive, blue eyed and non-sharp members of the staff. In the media houses, we typically praise the negative and mistake finding approach, not at least among the reporters. With this attitude, the media companies are about to cut their own throats as this culture cripples the creativity and performance of their employees."

When my wife completed her medical studies, she had to take a version of the Hippocratic Oath and, along with her fellow students, promise to "use my abilities with diligence and care, and to the benefit of society as a whole and my fellow men." When my class completed our training as journalists, we had a beer.

Whilst I was the chairman of the Centre for Journalism at the

University of Southern Denmark, the then journalist fellow and subsequent managing director of the Danish newspaper, Information, and cultural editor at Politiken, Mette Davidsen-Nielsen, worked with the then head of the program, Troels Mylenberg, who is now the editor-in-chief of the regional new chain Jysk Fynske Media, on the text of a journalistic oath, which we thought of as the equivalent to the doctor's Hippocratic Oath. In 2008, we put it like this:

Journalistic Oath

"In my work as a journalist I hereby undertake that I persistently and with an open mind will seek out and communicate the best achievable version of the truth.

My journalism is a societal duty. I am aware of my democratic responsibility, and my duty to hold those in power to account. For this reason, I will follow my conscience, and be both fair and self-critical.

My journalism will be both independent and even-handed, and I will be open about my methods. I will strive to present material with a sense of proportion, prioritise what is significant and make journalism comprehensible, interesting and relevant.

I know that I risk making mistakes, but I will recognise them and learn from them. Additionally, it is my ambition to seek out new paths and to contribute to journalistic development."

The journalistic oath was controversial, especially amongst those journalists who specialise in communication or pure entertainment. Today, journalism graduates are not asked to take an oath, but this kind of commitment is incorporated in the course training, and accordingly permeates the values with which they are educated. However, both new and experienced journalists could try to commit themselves more.

Journalism – That's Why

There is plenty of inspiration in the speech by former American Pre-sident Barack Obama in 2009 at the annual dinner for journalists who cover Washington politics daily. Seldom have the free press' challenges and its exponents' duty to the democratic process been formulated so clearly:

"I may not agree with everything you write or report. You help all of us who serve at the pleasure of the American people do our jobs better by holding us accountable, by demanding honesty, by preven-ting us from taking shortcuts and falling into easy political games that people are so desperately weary of. And that kind of reporting is worth preserving – not just for your sake, but for the public's. We count on you to help us make sense of a complex world and tell the stories of our lives the way they happen."

The press' dilemma is not between being controlling or being con-structive. It should be both. In addition to having a duty to make the significant relevant, fair and without showing preference, we have a duty to ask critical questions about the challenges that face our society and its people. We should also dare to inspire solutions and, on occasion, provide a framework within which those responsible for addressing them can do so.

So, ladies and gentlemen of the press, we need to change our at-titudes. Not just to save journalism from obsolescence in the form of bad habits and a tabloid culture which is not even effective as enter-tainment anymore, but also so that journalism can serve the society it is part of. For that to happen, we editors and news reporters will have to remember that it is our job to generate meaning. That good news can be about something good, something that works, something that we can learn from, and something that will make us smarter and inspire us.

The American reporter and author, David Bornstein, is still able to see his profession from the outside as his background is not traditional journalism education, but rather computer science and humanitarian aid. He has written the book How to Change the World, which focuses on social entrepreneurship, because he missed the good stories in the traditional media. He also co-founded the Solution Journalism Network in America with the ambition to inspire more journalism that engages in meaningful conversation.

"The majority of publishers, editors and reporters contend that the primary role of journalism is to expose wrongdoing," Bornstein explains.

"The general public also supports this function. But, today, along with all the other changes in media, it's fair to say that what is sometimes called solutions journalism should be seen as a legitimate branch of reporting; one that needs to be held to the same standards of accuracy and professionalism as other forms – rather than seen as a kind of fluffy feel-good feature to be offered, say, during the holiday season." His definition of journalism is the best I have heard:

"Journalism is a feedback mechanism to help society self-correct."

"We know from behavioural science that information about a problem alone is rarely sufficient to generate corrective action. People need to know what they can do – and how. That doesn't mean including a little 'good news' now and then, but regularly presenting people with innovative ideas and realistic pathways and possibilities that remain outside their view frame. In this sense, solutions journalism needs to be interwoven with traditional journalism – it rounds out the story, so to speak. Without it, society suffers."

Constructive News – Back Then

The American journalist Walter Lippmann published his book Public Opinion in 1922, in which he noted:

"The way in which the world is imagined determines at any particular moment what men will do."

The big publishers of the American press in the late 19th and early 20th century, Joseph Pulitzer and Randolph Hearst, would both agree as they became successful partly because they believed that their papers should be engaged in not only covering, but also facilitating and engaging in public debates on how to solve the problems facing the communities in which their publications were being published. But according to Peter Bro, professor in journalism from the University of Southern Denmark, this approach to journalism vanished during the course of the 20th century. Both Pulitzer and Hearst crossed the line from being only publishers to becoming politicians and engaged themselves and their papers directly in party politics. In order to gain more trust from the general public, alleged independent news publications in both America and Europe began to separate editorial view points from the journalistic content.

"Editors and reporters found it more meaningful to ask the elected leaders in the democracies what they would do to solve the problems of society rather than engage ordinary citizens," Bro explains, and continues that "In the last decades of the 20th century, a mixture of idealism and commercialism made more and more journalists and editors on both sides of the Atlantic experiment with new forms of journalism where citizens again were involved, and where media actively tried to help their communities to solve their problems."

The experiments had names like public journalism, civic journalism, solution-based journalism, citizen journalism, and many other terms – all with the intention to promote more problem-solving reporting.

"International research has singled out Denmark as a country where the press has tried to experiment with new forms, and new norms, of news publishing, and the work with constructive journalism demonstrates that this work now continues," Bro states.

Remember the DNA

In times of constant and rapid change in technologies, distribution channels, and financial models, it is more important than ever to remember the values, the role, and the foundation of truly good journalism. Christiane Amanpour of CNN put it brilliantly in her keynote to the NewsXchange conference in Morocco in November 2013:

"There is no substitute to the professional journalists who have spent their lives studying, working, doing, collecting wisdom, experience, and credibility. When people look at us – whoever gives them their news, they want to know one thing: Do these persons know what they are talking about, can I trust them, is this true, is it accurate? We mustn't give that away, thinking the future belongs to social media. Social media is fantastic, the amount of information we can get. But social media isn't journalism. It is information. Journalism is what we do with it. So we must believe in our own function. If we don't believe in us, nobody else will. We have to carry that flag, that torch of accurate, credible, experienced, trustworthy sources that people can turn to in order to know what is going on ... But we must remember to balance our cynicism."

In 2001, the great American news editors Bill Kovach and Tom Rosenstiel published the book The Elements of Journalism.

There they call the purpose of journalism not defined by technology, nor by journalists or the techniques they employ:

"News is that part of communication that keeps us informed of the changing events, issues, and characters in the world outside. Though it may be interesting or even entertaining, the foremost value of news is as a utility to empower the informed. The purpose of journalism is thus to provide citizens with the information they need to make the best possible decisions about their lives, their communities, their societies, and their governments."

Nothing in that definition contradicts with the vision of constructive journalism. And it might not be easy to find the balance while insisting on the essence of journalism to do good in the world, to be critical and constructive at the same time, and to tell important, engaging and inspirational stories.

But let us dare to promise naively like the children's TV character Bob the Builder, who had his slogan so cruelly stolen by a former American President: "Can we fix it? Yes, we can."

Exercise

Try to combine these 9 dots with only 4 straight lines without lifting the pen from the paper:

Give up? See the solution on the next page.

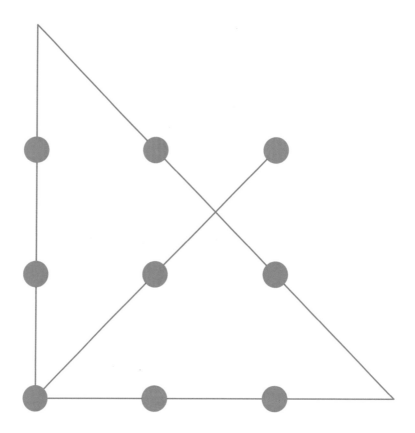

The solution is to think outside the box. Not to let traditional frames and habits limit your thinking.

Chapter 8

MIND YOUR STEP

When the wind of change blows, some people build windbreaks, others build windmills.

Old Chinese saying

No matter if you are a journalist, an editor, a politician or just a concerned citizen longing for a change in your daily newsfeed, and by now you think that there is some truth in this book, you will soon be engaged in several discussions with yourself, your colleagues, editors and people both on the inside and the outside of the media.

Here is a shortlist of the booby traps of constructive news that you should be aware of.

It is not positive news. Do not misunderstand that constructive news is the same as positive news. It is not. Constructive news criticises traditional news journalism where you only see the world with one eye. It does not argue that it is better to just see it with the other eye. Instead, good journalism is seeing the world with both eyes and with the ambition of providing the best obtainable version of the truth in order to engage people to make up their own minds.

Do not be a politician. Do not cross the line of subjectivity. Constructive news argues that a good story can be inspirational and that journalism can facilitate a better public debate on possible solutions to the problems facing society. But it is not the job of any professional journalist to define what the right solution is. That would be turning journalism into activism or pure politics. But just as professional journalists can facilitate a public debate on problems, we can facilitate a debate on how to solve them. And just as journalists can look for bad examples, we can also look for good examples.

Critical reporting is still important. Any dictator and other opponent of critical watchdog journalism will misuse the idea of constructive news and agree that there is far too much negative reporting and that a more constructive approach in coverage is necessary. Constructive news is not an alternative to the important role of the press to ask critical questions to people with power on behalf of the public. It is not a substitute for investigative reporting trying to dig beneath the polished surface of corrupt politicians, cynical CEOs or powerful interest groups. Constructive news is a supplement to, and a correction of, mainstream news journalism. It argues against the growing belief that in order to avoid criticism, one must have a critical approach to any civic authority, and when meeting people, doing so with skepticism and the notion that everything is bad, negative, corrupt and to be mistrusted.

It is not happy news. Constructive news is neither the North Korean approach to journalism, where problems are ignored and the sky is always blue. Nor is it the cute story of puppies riding skateboards on YouTube or the heartwarming report about the firefighter bringing down the little kitten from the big tree just before the weather report.

It is not conservative. Skeptics argue that constructive news is conservative by nature, and protects society from attack from more liberal or even revolutionary groups. This is not the case. Constructive news is not political. It is also not political to do journalism on a better tomorrow, as long as journalism does not define what better is.

Easy for you to say. Editors and reporters working in areas of the world with fundamental problems such as wars, hunger, child mortality etc., will argue that constructive news is much easier to practice for news media published in welfare states, such as the Scandinavian countries where international studies consistently find the happiest populations in the world. There is some truth in that, as the idea behind constructive news does not encourage ignoring the coverage of important problems. And having many important problems to focus on is indeed an easy excuse for failing to find the time, resources or news space to be constructive. But the bigger the problems, the greater the need to create meaning for the public by facilitating a debate on how to deal with those problems. Find best practice examples. Inspire hope. Find the light in the dark. Remember the definition of news is something out of the ordinary. So when the ordinary is trouble, the news is where the trouble has stopped.

Take care of too strict quantity goals. In South Africa, the new government appointed director general of the public service broadcaster SABC began his carrier by demanding of the news reporters, that 80 percent of the news coverage of South Africa should be positive. Probably he just agreed with the premise of this book that his news people missed a lot of the good stories out there. But because he was appointed by the government led by ANC, it was very easy to criticise him for trying to create more positive coverage of his political friends.

It is a both-and. The Americans have a nice expression called "The Tyranny of the OR", which explains the rhetorical trick that is often used to shoot down new ideas or viewpoints. Do you think form or content is the most important? Are you critical or constructive? Do you prefer black or white? Are you positive or negative? If you do not pay attention then you feel pressured to make a choice. However, the alternative to "The Tyranny of the OR" is "The Genius of the AND". Constructive news is not an alternative to critical reporting; it is a supplementary new tool in the editorial tool box.

Don't give up. Experiment with new ideas, new questions, new angles, and new ways. Find out what works, and what needs to be corrected. Find peers, share examples, use best practice.

Chapter 9

NOW WHAT?

If you are a reporter who wants to persuade your editor to give way to more constructive news, try the argument of experiment:

- Try to add a constructive angle on your next story, and monitor the reactions from your readers, viewers, and listeners. Share the experience.
- Find a likeminded person inside (or outside) the newsroom.
- Conduct a workshop where you look at the stories you have made today. How many of them deal with conflicts, drama, crooks or victims? Ask: would you read/watch it yourself if you were not paid to do so? Will your children or neighbours? Look at the stories again: How could you add constructive angles by looking for ways out, best practice or facilitate a debate on how to deal with the problem? How could you involve your audience?
- Suggest to your editor and colleagues that you try just to publish one constructive story. Next week suggest that you try for one day or in one section to look for solutions and not only problems, just to learn.
- Praise: Editors are human too. They would love to be told that they have guts and vision. And they in fact need to be reminded that they are journalists as well, who can deal with important stories to the benefit of society instead of all the budget cuts, union meetings and management-rhetoric that steal their time and engagement.

If you are an editor trying to motivate your reporters to be more constructive:

- Show them the declining circulation figures/ratings. Again. But this time, ask them the question: Don't you think that we probably will end up with more of the same result if we continue doing what we have always done?
- Show them the principles of constructive news and quote former skeptical and skilled reporters who have realised that it is possible to be both critical and constructive. Invite speakers, or visit other newsrooms who have tried this.
- Experiment: Workshops, The Day of Yes, a Good News Section, a series involving the community to come up with ideas to solve the problem your reporters have documented.
- Praise behaviour, ideas and stories you want more of. Give rewards to the best constructive angle.
- Tell your audience about your plans. And invite them to give feedback along the way.
- Post all the positive reactions you begin to receive from readers, viewers and neighbours. And don't forget to share when your daughter suddenly voluntarily spends time reading/watching one of your stories.
- Think about why your audience loves your daily weather report. You might hate it as much as your hard-hitting newsroom thinking it's not really journalism. But what makes the weather forecast different and so relevant for people? It's not only about today or yesterday: It deals with the weather tomorrow and in the weekend. What if you also used data and experts to do stories on tomorrow on other areas in your community: Demographics, schools, traffic, crime, health, etc.
- Make your own version of the new BBC program "My Perfect Country", where listeners share ideas on how the community can improve and three experts debate, which of the ideas of improvement would make most sense.

If you are a politician hoping for reporters to begin to change their behaviour and give you more airtime.

- Don't bother. Concentrate on yourself. What about saying what you really mean, instead of what your spin doctor tells you would be smart to say? What about spending time on coming up with good ideas to solve the problems facing society, instead of looking for weak arguments from your opponent.
- Send this book to a newsroom near you. Anonymously.

Be constructive.
Share your experience.
Good luck.

Takeaway

Constructive Journalism is

- critical, objective, and balanced
- tackling important issues facing society, not trivial
- unbiased
- calm in its tone and does not give in to scandals and outrage
- bridging, not polarising
- forward-looking and future-oriented
- nuanced and contextualised
- based on facts
- facilitating well-informed debate around solutions to well documented
- problems

Constructive Journalism is Not

- promoting a specific agenda, crossing the line between journalism and politics
- uncritical or naive
- promoting heroes, governments or civil society organisations
- obscuring critical viewpoints
- activism in any shape or form
- dumbed-down, trivial or happy news
- giving in to false equivalence/balance
- proposing solutions to problems or advocating one solution over another
- over-simplifying complex problems or solutions to complex problems

Chapter 10

JOIN THE GLOBAL MOVEMENT

"Nothing is as powerful, as an idea whose time has come."

Victor Hugo, Author

Ignaz Semmelweis was not a popular man among his fellow doctors.

In the mid-19th century, before the germ theory of disease was confirmed, it was not unusual for doctors to go directly from an autopsy procedure to the maternity ward to deliver babies, and the new mothers were dying from childbed fever.

While working at an Obstetrical Clinic in Vienna, Semmelweis noticed that doctors' wards had three times the mortality compared to the midwives' wards, and tried to convince doctors they were killing their own patients because they were not washing their hands. Some doctors were offended at the suggestion that they themselves were causing their patients' deaths. Dr. Semmelweis' ideas were rejected, he became severely depressed, had a breakdown, was admitted to a mental asylum, and died only 14 days later, aged 47, after a particularly bad beating by the guards.

A journalist admitting that news people are not doing our job well enough and in fact are doing harm to democracy, does not win popularity contests among peers either.

Isn't it a betrayal of the profession and destroying the credibility of professional men and women having a hard time already and doing their best?

Isn't it in fact better for the public if this criticism could take place behind closed doors, as people do need someone to trust, and an open debate on the fact that we can improve will destroy that trust?

Sir Martyn Lewis is well aware of how controversial it is to speak out about journalism.

In the 1980s, he was the most respected and well-known news anchor at the BBC in London. But he became increasingly frustrated with the news he was presenting to the British public evening after evening. Not that it was fake news, but the news anchor just didn't feel that the picture he presented was right.

"We told so many negative stories, though the world was much more nuanced," Sir Martyn Lewis recalls. He tried to talk with his editors and colleagues, but they refused to listen. News was news.

In 1993, he was invited to give a talk in Los Angeles, and he decided to speak out, far away from London. But to make sure he was on the safe side, he had the communications director of the BBC go through his speech before he left.

"It was not easy. I could not mention that I thought that we journalists and also the BBC were not giving a fair and accurate picture of the world. But in the end, we agreed that instead of mentioning the BBC, I could say "a TV station close to my heart."

When Lewis landed in LAX airport in Los Angeles, he was being asked by the ground personnel to contact his bosses at home.

"On the phone I was being told, if I held that speech, I would be fired. I got so mad, that I said that they couldn't fire me, because I felt I no longer worked at the BBC, which normally fought for freedom of expression and public good."

Lewis did his speech, which was reported by CNN and international media, and when he returned days later, he thought he should clear his desk at the BBC. Instead he was invited for coffee by his bosses, who didn't dare fire him: Thousands of viewers had contacted the BBC to tell that they fully supported their news anchor. They too found that their evening news was far too negative.

Lewis stayed in his job through most of the 90s.

But he left without seeing a change in the news culture and news content.

Sir Martyn, who has chaired the National Council for Voluntary Organisations in Great Britain, told me his story the day after I had

CONSTRUCTIVE INSTITUTE – JOURNALISM FOR TOMORROW

Vision — Improve democracy and public knowledge

Mission — Make journalism great again

Goals — Change the global news culture in five years

Strategies — Provide new knowledge, new inspiration and new ambassadors of constructive news

Tactics — Non profit funding to create a global constructive journalistic movement

Action plans — Constructive Institute at Aarh. Uni. Fellows, Conference, research Partnerships / global hubs

Source: Constructive Institute 2017

made a talk at the BBC Newsroom in 2016. The fact that the BBC now listened and even now has decided to include so called "Solution-Focused Journalism" in its core news strategy gives him hope:

"It came late, but I do hope there is now more awareness of the fact that we do need to change our negative culture in the news business."

So, the diagnosis that news culture is ill is not new. What is new is that more and more agree, and that the idea of constructive news as a medicine with the potential to cure the patient, now spreads around the world. And more and more newsrooms find that constructive news does not cripple any of the virtues on which great journalism must stand. The key elements of good journalism as expressed by the great American editors Tom Rosenstiel and Bill Kovach, whose work on journalism and leadership I enjoyed during my year at Stanford University in the early 90s are as follows:

1. Journalism's first **obligation** is to the **truth**.
2. Its first **loyalty** is to **citizens**
3. Its essence is a **discipline** of **verification**.
4. Its practitioners must maintain an **independence** from those they cover.
5. It must serve as an **independent monitor** of **power**.

6. It must provide a forum for public **criticism** and **compromise**.
7. It must strive to make the **significant interesting** and **relevant**.
8. It must keep the news **comprehensive** and **proportional**.
9. Its practitioners must be allowed to exercise their **personal conscience**.

Constructive journalism builds exactly on those old principles. Not on activism. Not on subjectivity. Not on journalists taking the roles of politicians.

Commit Yourself

On March 1st, 2017, I had been heading DR News for ten years and enjoying every moment of it. A better mission, a better newsroom, better journalists and a more important task as an editor-in-chief you cannot get in Denmark – or maybe elsewhere.

But the vision of constructive journalism is to me so important for not only journalism and news media, but also for democracy itself, that I just had to commit myself to it.

On September 1st, 2017, we launched Constructive Institute as an independent non-profit organisation placed right on campus of Aarhus University. On our board serves the former EU commissioner Connie Hedegaard, media director of the European Broadcasting Union in Geneva Jean Philip De Tender, the chairman of UN Live and former CEO of Huffington post Jimmy Maymann, Aarhus University representative Head of Communication Anders Correll, the former editor-in-chief and now member of the board of the regional media house Fynske Media, Per Westergård, myself and lawyer Steffen Ebdrup of the press foundation, Aarhus Stiftstidendes Fond.

We have an advisory board with equally fantastic people like:
- Michael Moeller, director general at the United Nations Office at Geneva, Switzerland
- Peter Bro, professor of journalism at the Centre for Journalism in University of Southern Denmark, Denmark

- Dawn Garcia, director of the John S. Knight Fellowships Program at Stanford University, United States
- Espen Egil Hansen, editor-in-chief at Aftenposten, Norway
- Rasmus Kleis Nielsen, associate professor at Reuters Institute for the Study of Journalism, United Kingdom
- Jesper Højberg, executive director of International Media Support
- Anne Lagercrantz, director of news at SVT, Sweden
- Trine Nielsen, director of education and knowledge at the Danish School of Media and Journalism, Denmark
- Johann Oberauer, CEO of Oberauer Publishing, Austria
- Erik Rasmussen, founder of Global Think Tank Sustainia, Denmark
- Richard Sambrook, director of the Cardiff School of Journalism, Media and Cultural Studies at Cardiff University, and former director of BBC News, United Kingdom

Based on philanthropy, and supported so far by TrygFonden, Bestseller, Den Fynske Bladfond, Aarhus Stiftstidendes Fond and Helsinki Sanomat, the idea is to use Denmark and media in Northern Europe as a showcase and spread best practice to the rest of the world.

We follow three roads:

1. **New knowledge**, which is why we are placed at Aarhus University, where Rector Brian Bech Nielsen heads his university of 40,000 students based on the vision that a university serves not only its students, by also society with new knowledge, which can lead to solutions of the challenges faced by civilisation. We want to interact with independent researchers at Aarhus University and elsewhere to find evidence on how news media influence not only democracy and politics, but also the human mind – and if we do it differently, what is the impact? We want to help future journalists with new educational material on constructive journalism. We want to invent new creative constructive media formats and share it with the news industry.

2. **New inspiration**. We want to share ideas, best practices and motivational insights at conferences, seminars, keynotes, master classes, workshops and give out global constructive prizes. We will help boards of media companies find new strategies and help editors implement new culture and new storytelling. We will build a database with best practice examples and share information and be part of the growing constructive movement via social media, our own website and partnerships. In five years, we aim to be – alone or with partners – present with hubs in Europe, North America, Asia and Africa.

3. **New role models**. Six Constructive Fellows started at the end of August 2017 as journalistic talents to broaden their minds at Aarhus University, where they not only can update their knowledge and in depth understanding of the challenges facing society on their beat, but also look for possible solutions for society. Meanwhile, we give them training in constructive journalism. After a full academic year of 10 months they return to their news organisations as role models and agents of change for better journalism at Politiken, Fyens Stiftstidende, Kristeligt Dagblad, Jysk-Fynsk Medier and DR News. The fellowship program, which is inspired by the John S. Knight Fellowship Program at Stanford University and the Nieman Fellowship at Harvard, has English as its working language and will, from 2018, consist of 6 Danish and 6-8 international journalists and editors.

Yes, we need help to do all this. Partners and funders to supplement our partners like the United Nations, the World Association of Newspapers and News Publishers (WAN-IFRA), the International News Media Association, the European Broadcasting Union, all three Danish Journalism education institutions, media organisations like Politiken, TV2, Kristeligt Dagblad, Mediehusene Midtjylland, Deutche Welle, Google, Facebook, and our early funders like Aarhus Stiftstidende Foundation, Den Fynske Bladfond, TrygFonden and Bestseller.

The experienced investigative Danish reporter Orla Borg, the Oxford educated Maarja Kadajane who who has been working with international media – at the EBU and elsewhere – for over ten years, and political scientist Peter Damgaard Kristensen heading our small staff at Constructive Institute look forward to hearing from you, if you have ideas, want to support us, or be part of the global movement. Go to our website for more information at constructiveinstitute.org.

Why do we think, we can do this?

- The crisis in the media business is now so obvious that no company can stone wall constructive criticism any longer.
- More and more young reporters want a change in journalism.
- This criticism does not come from the outside; from politicians, big business or interest groups, which makes it easy to ignore for an independent press used to fighting any outside pressure. It comes from editors, publishers and journalists out of a worry and love for journalism and with the ambition to make journalism great again.
- New constructive groups of reporters or networks for solutions focused journalism are spreading, and the demand for common standards, definitions and vocabulary is only growing.
- Invitations to Constructive Institute to do keynotes, seminars and workshops come from news organisations from all over the word.
- And media owners find the vision of constructive news meaningful. When I made a keynote at "The INMA Global News Media Congress" in New York in May 2017, 424 CEOs from news media from 42 countries rose from their seats and applauded – most likely because they were so happy that I finally stopped talking. But maybe also because they understood after just another conference about the future of news and depressing demands of investment in data analyses, new platforms, new apps, and new distribution channels, that constructive news is a cheap strategy which is more about changing mindset and changing bad habits of just running faster, instead of agreeing to where to run to.

The time is right. The time is now. We need to experiment. We need to share ideas. We need to generate new knowledge. We need a global movement of opportunity, hope and courage to think differently. And we cannot wait any longer for *somebody* to do *something sometime*.

We are the change, we are waiting for.

THE NEED FOR MEDIA EMPOWERMENT

By Michael Møller

Director-General of the United Nations Office in Geneva

Whether through newspapers, social media or broadcast, media empower us all. They empower us by bringing us stories that matter to our daily lives, alerting us to the trends that are changing our world, engaging us in debate, and holding decision-makers to account. We need data, we need different points of view, we need to see solutions that inspire us to action. That is the bedrock of democracy and of progress. Are we getting that?

In Ulrik Haagerup's analysis we are not. I agree. And I firmly believe it is critical that we figure out a way to ensure that we do.

We live in a world where the flow of information and the possibilities for citizen participation have never been greater. Yet, many feel disempowered by the news, are disappointed in their political leadership and disengaged from decision-making. This generates a democratic deficit through apathy and indifference.

This concerns us as individuals but is also fundamental to how we shape a better world collectively. The information we get determines our choices. And more than ever, we need to make the sustainable and long-term choices. We cannot afford a one-dimensional view of the world that ignores complexity and glosses over connections across challenges.

It is a debate of vital importance to the United Nations, and to all of us: freedom of expression and access to knowledge are essential in our efforts to promote peace, rights and well-being for all. In world of more than 7 billion people, with a cacophony of voices that are often ill-informed and based on narrow agendas, we need media that take seriously the responsibility to educate and serve as a counter-point to power.

Because we increasingly witness how rules are broken with impunity: ongoing and fresh conflicts, young girls kidnapped and held hostage, waste dumped into our oceans, journalists silenced, passenger planes blown out of the sky, eavesdropping and censorship, the list goes on. Leadership entails an important level of global responsibility.

But if the Security Council fails to act on breaches of international peace and security, how can we expect others to respect the rules?

There is no stability without solidarity, and no solidarity without stability. We need a return to common decency, and this will only come if our leaders set an example that we can follow. This is why we need responsible media that empower. We simply need constructive alternatives in the current stream of news.

Ulrik Haagerup is at the forefront of fresh thinking about the role of the media in today's world and how to bring us those alternatives. It is often said that we get the media and the political leaders we deserve. It is our shared responsibility to ensure that we get the best. Because that is how we are all empowered. "Constructive News" is a welcome call for a more profound reflection about priorities and choices, not just among media professionals and political leaders, but for all of us.

WANT TO KNOW MORE?

Ackoff, R. L. (1999). *Re-Creating the Corporation: A Design of Organizations for the 21st Century.*

Barrett, F. J., & Fry, R. E. (2005). *Appreciative Inquiry: A Positive Approach to Building Cooperative Capacity.*

Barlett, D. L., & Steele, J. B. (1992). *America: What Went Wrong?*

Carlson, C. R., & Wilmot, W. W. (2006). *Innovation: The Five Disciplines for Creating What Customers Want.*

Christensen, J. L. & Lundvall, B. (2004). Research on Technological Innovation, Management and Policy (vol. 8: Product Inovation [sic], Interactive Learning and Economic Performance).

Collins, J. (2001). *Good to Great: Why Some Companies Make the Leap and Others Don't.*

Coyle, D. (2012). *The Little Book of Talent: 52 Tips for Improving Your Skills.*

Day, G. S., & Schoemaker, P. J. H. (2006). *Peripheral Vision: Detecting the Weak Signals That Will Make or Break Your Company.*

Diamandis, P. H., & Kotler, S. (2012). *Abundance: The Future is Better Than You Think.*

Dixon, P. (2003). *Futurewise: Six Faces of Global Change.*

Fisher, R., Ury, W. L., & Patton, B. (2011). *Getting to Yes: Negotiating Agreement Without Giving In.*

Florida, R. (2002). *The Rise of the Creative Class: And How It's Transforming Work, Leisure, Community and Everyday Life.*

Friedman, G. (2009). *The Next 100 Years: A Forecast for the 21st Century.*

Gardner, H. E., Csikszentmihalyi, M., & Damon, W. (2001). *Good Work: When Excellence and Ethics Meet.*

Gladwell, M. (2013). *David and Goliath: Underdogs, Misfits, and the Art of Battling Giants.*

Grant, A. (2013). *Give and Take: Why Helping Others Drives Our Success.*

Greider, W. (1992). *Who Will Tell the People: The Betrayal of American Democracy.*

Hendricks, V. F. (2014). *Infostorm: How to Take Information Punches and Save Democracy.*

Hendricks, V. F., & Hansen, P. G. (2016). Infostorms: Why do we 'like'? Explaining individual behavior on the social net. (2nd ed.).

Isaacson, W. (2012). *The Real Leadership Lessons of Steve Jobs. Harvard Business Review, 90*(4), 92-102.

McAlpine, A. (2000). *The Ruthless Leader: Three Classics of Strategy and Power.*

Prahalad, C. K. & Krishnan, M. S. (2008). *The New Age of Innovation: Driving Cocreated Value Through Global Network.*

Rosenstiel, T., Just, M., Belt, T. L., Pertilla, A., Dean, W., & Chinni, D. (2007). *We Interrupt This Newscast: How to Improve Local News and Win Ratings, Too.*

Rosling, H. *Don't Panic* – www.gapminder.org

Schatz, R., & Vollbracht, M. (2010). *Trust Meltdown; The Financial Industry Needs a Fundamental Restart.*

Schudson, M. (1982). *The Power of News.*

Siegel, M. (2005). *False Alarm: The Truth about the Epidemic of Fear.*

Speculand, R. (2003). *Turning It On: Surefire Business Stories to Ignite, Excite and Entertain.*

Sutton, R. I. (2010). *Good Boss, Bad Boss: How to Be the Best ... and Learn from the Worst.*

Useem, M. (2009). The Go Point: When It's Time to Decide--Knowing What to Do and When to Do It.

Wallace, J., & Erickson, J. (1993). *Hard Drive: Bill Gates and the Making of the Microsoft Empire.*

Young, J. S. & Simon, W. L. (2005). iCon: *Steve Jobs, the Greatest Second Act in the History of Business.*